Daughters of the King

Finding Your Place in the Bible Story

Melissa Deming

Daughters of the King: Finding Your Place in the Biblical Story
© 2013 by Melissa Deming

Book edited by Amanda Williams.

ACKNOWLEDGMENTS

Fresh-faced from seminary and a whopping overseas experience, I am thankful to the group of ladies who participated (more likely endured) my first Bible study. The women of University Baptist Church in San Antonio, Texas were both faithful and gracious to sit and listen for ten weeks as I bumbled through the original version of *Daughters of the King*. When I think of the other studies written by well-known authors they might have enjoyed during this time, I am overwhelmed that they continued to show up each week.

To my friends living overseas whom God used as the occasion to write this study, I miss you terribly, but I praise God that one day we will rejoice with the King together in his final kingdom. To my friend and webmaster, Nive Burris, who played an indelible role in challenging me to filter my own culture through the prism of God's Word, this book would not be the same without your penetrating questions and hard-won answers. And to my editor, friend, and the enabler of several of my bad habits, Amanda Williams, I will be forever grateful for your notes regarding both commas and clarity, as well as your constant encouragement to read and write. To Emily Whitten, thank you for your keen insight into the final shape of the book.

I am thankful to my parents, Sid and Diane King, who provided me with my first theological education by loving me and leading me to Christ. To my father who ensured my education came despite cost or space and my mother who first whispered to me that she thought I might be a writer one day, you are the largest earthly measures of any success I will find. To my two older and much more godly sisters, Heather Moore and Caroline Wear, thank you for reading this study and even trying it out on your own small group. I am indebted to you for more than just your supportive prayers and am supremely thankful for our special and prized relationship as best friends.

To my husband of nearly 12 years, Jonathan, who has listened and championed me, thank you for giving me room to do those things that make my heart sing the most and loudest. Being bound to you has resulted in more freedoms than I could possible imagine and offers a sweet shadow of the freedoms that will ultimately come with my union with Christ. I love you.

And last, to my sons, Zacharias King and Jonah Joseph, I hope this study doesn't embarrass you when you turn 16. But sometimes in parenting God gives us such reticent and universal examples of his love for us as his children that we simply must share. When you grow up, I pray you will grow up to be bold priests of God and valiant servants of the King. Nothing else matters.

INTRODUCTION

It was a miracle that I didn't knock anything over when I busted into the Christian bookstore. I was on a mission. I was stateside only for a week, and I had very little time to find a Bible study that explained the whole of the Bible from the very beginning – what it all meant and how it applied today.

After rifling through all the bookshelves and coming up empty-handed, I jumped on a salesperson for help. I think I dumped my whole story out on him in about three breaths.

While living in Southeast Asia, God had given me the thrilling opportunity to share my culture and my faith with some local friends. But after our initial conversations, I quickly realized the meager library I had shipped over from the states was lacking. I needed a comprehensive resource to share with them. I needed something 'big picture.' With no previous exposure to the gospel or the God of the Bible, I knew my friends would never come to faith if I just jumped into the story of the Bible in the middle. I needed to lay some groundwork before introducing them to Jesus.

Our worldviews differed, and I quickly discovered so should my approach. Hence, I became a crazed lady on a mission in a Christian bookstore.

You can imagine my disappointment when the salesperson informed me they carried no such study, not even a Bible in my friends' heart language. Having only a week and no time to order one, I went back overseas empty handed and heavy hearted.

Soon after, God led me to New Tribes Mission: a missions-sending organization with a powerful publishing arm. Their 48-week chronological Bible study, *Firm Foundations: Creation to Christ*, formed the basis of the Bible studies I would soon host with my local friends. Thankful to have a tool that started at the very beginning of the Bible and continued to the end, I still lamented that a more accessible study wasn't available on the market.

It is out of my time spent with my friends in Southeast Asia that *Daughters of the King: Finding Your Place in the Biblical Story* was born – a 10-week journey through the Bible.

In the years following my return to the United States, my home country has increasingly become a mission field in its own right. It wasn't long before books and resources on understanding the Bible as one, unified story began to dot the market. It is from this wealth of information that I undergirded *Daughters of the King*.

Originally written for my home church in San Antonio, Texas, *Daughters of the King* relies heavily on two sources: *God's Big Picture: Tracing the Storyline of the Bible* by Vaughan Roberts and *The Drama of Scripture* by Craig Bartholomew. In fact, the definition of the kingdom that I use in this study is taken verbatim from Vaughan Roberts' book, who in turn borrows from biblical theologian and story architect Graeme Goldsworthy. I am indebted to both these authors for blazing this interpretative trail.

So, what makes *Daughters of the King* different from these other valuable tools on the biblical story? *Daughters of the King* is the representation of my time spent overseas, engaging a different worldview and trying to strip the Bible down to its most basic storyline. You can see from the visuals, charts, and definitions that I cater to a reader with little or no formal training in the Bible, although this study would also be a refreshing read for long-time Christians who have lost their zeal for the loveliness of God's Word and still wonder at the relevance of this divinely-inspired Book.

As such, *Daughters of the King* is not simply a summary of the kingdom of God – what it is, who's a part of it, and God's purposes for creating it. Rather, *Daughters of the King* offers the reader a systematic look at how the Bible is arranged around the topic of God's kingdom and how God's kingdom applies to women. I trace the story of the King's kingdom by following the canonical divisions of the Scriptures – the Law (Torah), the Prophets and the Writings, the History Books, the Gospels, Acts, and the Epistles. The book of Revelation acts as a conclusion to this study.

Most importantly, through these divisions, I trace the concept of the promised Seed – a royal individual first pictured in Gen. 3:15 and anticipated throughout the entire biblical story. It is, after all, his kingdom that we step into when we read the story of the Bible.

Chapter 1 looks at God's original intention in setting up his kingdom (*Gen.*

1-2). In chapter 2 we see what went wrong in the world - how the King's subjects rebel against the throne (*Gen. 3*). Chapter 3 reveals the King's promise to rescue his servants from the consequences of their rebellion (*Gen. 4-49*). In chapter 4, the reader learns the King extends grace to his subjects in three ways: through the sacrificial system, the Law, and the tabernacle (*Exodus – Deuteronomy*). Chapter 5 looks at the kingdom from the view of the History Books and the demands of the King's subjects to be led by an earthly king (*Joshua – Esther*). In chapter 6, we close out the portion of the biblical story in the Old Testament by looking at the King's prophets – the men and their two-pronged message of judgment and hope (*Job - Malachi*).

We resume our birds-eye view of the biblical story in the New Testament with chapter 7 heralding the arrival of the promised King (*the Gospels*). Then in chapter 8, we welcome the arrival of the King's Helper – the Holy Spirit (*Acts*). In chapter 9, we discover the biblical story has a challenging, yet crucial role for each of us as the King's priests (*the Epistles*), and in the final chapter, we see the fulfillment of God's original goal for his kingdom, a kingdom at rest (*Revelation*).

To help women everywhere understand and better study the themes of the biblical story, I provide definitions or key truths for almost every chapter. These definitions are crucial because all of God's future promises are rooted in the notion of his kingdom and ultimately fulfilled in the identity of the individual the Bible calls the King. To help you apply the lessons in the book, I've created a free downloadable workbook with group discussion questions and individual study material. Please visit my website, http://hiveresources.com/book/, to find out how to receive your free copy.

While there are many Bible studies written by students more versed in the Scriptures than I, it is my hope that *Daughters of the King* speaks to you as a woman in Christ. The imagery of royalty commonly associated with this term easily evokes special privileges and an elevated status many crave, yet few realize comes with a price. I present *Daughters of the King* for women of all cultures, hoping it will help us all understand God's global mission for the nations and his heart for women to be servants of the King above all, regardless of where God's story takes us.

With all the King's love,

Melissa Deming

INTRODUCTION

CONTENTS

CHAPTER 1: THE KING'S KINGDOM
GENESIS 1-2

I have a confession: I am addicted to books - reading them, buying them, hoarding them, and yes, decorating with them. My color-coded bookshelves have been the cause of much derision among my friends. Most women buy shoes and makeup; I buy hardcovers and trade books. In fact, I think the last pair of shoes I bought was a pair of snow boots - a practical purchase after moving from Texas to the northeast. And I don't dare reveal the current state of my mascara. The good news is my little habit makes me a very cheap date, since all the romance I require is a tall Mocha and a trip to my local used bookstore. The bad news is my book-buying habit proves to be quite expensive at moving time. I think our church family is still taking Tylenol after they moved us across town, in the rain, a few years ago.

But if I were to isolate the root of my book-buying obsession, I'm inclined to think my love for books is really about my love for a good story.

And you know, we all have a story. Sometimes our stories are happy. Sometimes tragic. Sometimes our stories feature bravery, overcoming obstacles, and winning battles. More often they feature unexpected loss, sore regret, and gut-wrenching betrayal. Sometimes we are the main characters of our stories, while others often take center stage. And while each of our life stories is different, they all share one common thread: our stories all fall under the umbrella of God's story.

THE STORY OF THE KING

One Story

God has given us his story. It's his Word, but we often treat his Word like a collection of books on a dusty bookshelf. We take one off the shelf without any consideration for how it relates to the other books that are left behind.

Worse still, when we open one of those books, we read it in the strangest ways – one page at a time. You wouldn't consider ripping one page out of a library book, checking it out and taking it home to read would you?

If you were to check out one page at a time from the library – instead of the whole book – what good would it do you? Would you be able to tell me the plot of the book from just one page? What about even part of it – like the main conflict or the climactic event? Could you tell me about the characters? Does your single page reveal the protagonist's fatal flaw or the antagonist's tragic backstory? What about the ending and how the story finds resolution?

No. We would never read a novel that way. What about a letter from a friend? Would you rip out one paragraph and throw away the rest of the note? Again, no. You'd likely miss part of her message, and the next time you talked you'd need to spend time "catching up" all over again.

But this is how we often treat the biblical story. No wonder we have trouble applying God's Word to our lives. No wonder we have trouble figuring out where our story fits into God's story.

The Bible is intended to be one, unified story. Yes, we often read the books of the Bible separately. After all, it's comprised of 66 different books by 40 different authors covering 2,000 years of history. But each book plays an important part in the grand story, the grand biblical narrative.

In *Daughters of the King* we will look at that central theme of the Bible so that wherever you are in the biblical text, you will be able to pick out the central meaning and better apply it to your life. And for those who haven't spent much time studying or reading the Bible, I hope this book helps you discern and understand the importance of the Bible's overarching message: *that a good King created a good world, and although it was corrupted by sin, he is at work to completely restore it through his Son, Jesus Christ.*

One Author

The Bible is a unified story because it was all written by the same author. It is God's Word to man, meaning God directed men of different ages and cultures to write his message through his Spirit. That's the important part – through his Spirit.

Second Tim. 3:16-17 says: *"All Scripture is given by inspiration of God, and is profitable for doctrine, for reproof, for correction, for instruction in righteousness, that the man of God may be complete, thoroughly equipped for every good work."*[1]

So, while the Bible is both a human and divine book, it is a unified book.

One Message

Because of the Holy Spirit's role in the creation of the Bible, we can be assured that it has a unified theme, namely that salvation from sin comes through the Son of God. We see shadows of the faith in the promised Messiah even in the Old Testament!

This is why we'll be spending a considerable bit of time in the Old Testament because there is no disunity between it and the New. Jesus himself said, *"...these are the Scriptures that testify about me" (John 5:39)*. At the time Jesus spoke, the New Testament had not yet been written. So, he could only be referring to the Law, Writing, and the Prophets of the Hebrew Scriptures. Additionally, when Jesus and the apostles quote Scripture in the New Testament, they are quoting from the Old! (cf. Luke 24:44)

Above all, I want you to be assured of these things:

Scripture is coherent. It tells one story in which there are no contradictions. This is important to note because as we encounter difficult texts, we will be following a specific method of interpretation. We will let Scripture interpret Scripture – not our culture, not our circumstances, not our own feelings.

Scripture is reliable. It is a divine book in which we can place our trust.

Scripture is relevant. If the Bible is the story of God's activity in the world, then it applies to everyone! You can hold fast to the reality that God is at work in your life!

So, let's start in the very beginning - Genesis 1 - and dive right into the biblical story. If you're using the workbook that goes with this book, pull it out and start taking notes!

THE KING'S RULE

God created a good creation

Read Genesis 1:1-3. Keep your eye out for the number of times God declares his creation "good." God declares his artistry "good" seven times!

Do you think the author is trying to communicate something? God's creation is good; it mirrors his goodness

Read Genesis 1:26-31.

God's goal for creation is rest

Read Genesis 2:1-3.

The creation event culminated in a state of rest. In the text, the fact that God rested is mentioned twice in these verses. In fact, God even had a place in mind where man was to experience this rest: a lush, lovely garden.

Read Genesis 2:7-25. Look carefully at Gen. 2:8, *"Now the LORD God had planted a garden in the east, in Eden; and there he put the man he had formed."*

Sometimes our English translations aren't always able to capture the full textures of the biblical story. In Gen. 2:15, the word "put" is different than what is used in Gen. 2:8. In verse 8, the word "put" (Heb. *suwm*) is commonly used to indicate putting or even appointing to a place. But in verse 15, the author uses a different word (Heb. *yanach)*, which means literally "to rest – settle down or remain." This nuance speaks to God's intention in creating a place for Adam to dwell. In a very purposeful way, God "rested" Adam in the garden.

So, we see that the first kingdom was restful. The first restful life involved man and woman living in harmony with their holy King, with each other, and with the whole created order.

God's rule over creation brings blessing

To live under God's rule means to enjoy his blessing.[2]

In various cultures, the terms 'authority' and 'rule' have negative meanings. Depending on your background it is really easy to think of 'rule' as the reign of a tyrant. And don't we often perceive God to be that way?

God, where were you when _____ happened? Why did you sit by and allow _____ to hurt me? God, why did you bless her with _____, and not me? Why are you withholding _____ from me?

You can fill in whatever blank you're staring at in your life right now. In the midst of difficulty, it is all too easy to view God's commandments or life prescriptives as inconvenient or restrictive or even unfair.

But the rule of God, as originally intended in the garden, is the only way we can fully experience life and blessing – to be at peace and have rest.

In fact, the idea of "abundant life" that we hear in the New Testament only comes when we are living in God's kingdom and under his rule and experiencing the blessings that come with his kingdom.

Check out the definition for the kingdom of God and its significance. These definitions are crucial because all of God's future promises are going to be rooted in the notion of His kingdom.

DEFINITION: **The kingdom of God** – is God's people in God's place under God's rule and blessing.[3]

SIGNIFICANCE: The kingdom of God is God's pattern for a restful life - man living at peace with God, each other, and all creation.

Look at Gen. 1-2, Adam and Eve had everything they needed for a happy life. They had a perfect relationship with God, a perfect home, and perfect relationships with each other. That sounds like a dream doesn't it? That is what God still envisions for you and me today!

In the first kingdom we see what kind of life God intended for us to live. God intended for life in His kingdom to be restful, characterized by harmony with God, each other, and all his creation.

Think on your life right now? Would you call it restful? I'm not asking if you're *physically rested*. When my boys were younger, they napped twice a day! As an adult, I can only imagine how productive I might be if I was guaranteed at least one nap a day. Typically, I'm just praying no one wakes me up in the middle of the night. Too often I awaken at 3:00 am with a pair of beady little eyes peering at me from over the sheets. Sometimes I don't even have to open my eyes because I can hear them breathing like Darth Vadar. Moms everywhere know what I'm talking about. If you have young children at home or even work with children during the day, you are probably not physically rested.

I'm also not asking if your life is *emotionally rested*. In any given week, my schedule always gets the best of me. Seriously, it can beat me up and tear me down faster than anything else in my life. But even in the everyday moments of life, we battle tension and stress. In fact, if I'm going to create any quiet or restful place in my house, it usually can only be found in the bathroom. And even then, there are fingers waving at me from under the door. Stress. One way or another it's going to find you and weasel its little fingers under the door of your most sacred place!

So, what am I saying when I ask if your life is restful? I'm asking if you're *spiritually rested.* Are you at peace regardless of your circumstances or season of life? Or would you say your life is defined by fear? Do you lie at wake at night with thoughts that won't quit? Are you so overcome with regret and sorrow over a situation with a specific individual that you cannot, no matter how hard you try, take the next step in your life? Do you spend way more time than is necessary trying to carve out a place for yourself at the office, in the dorm, in your marriage, that every little event blows you out the water? A bad conversation? It will consume you for weeks. Ignored or slighted by a friend? It will send you out of orbit. Recovering from setbacks seems impossible

That's not the type of life God envisioned for Adam when he 'rested' him there in the garden. God had another kind of life in mind, and he does for you, too.

The author of Genesis will continue to unpack the meaning of 'restful' for us. But by 'restful' God clearly does not mean that man should be stress-free or solely dedicated to leisure. Rather, God gave the man and woman specific tasks as they lived as his subjects.

So, let's look at what you and I are to be doing in the King's 'restful' kingdom.

THE KING'S SUBJECTS

Read Genesis 1:26-27 again.

God creates man and woman in a different way than the rest of creation; God is involved in a more personal way. Notice the text says *"Let Us make"* rather than the impersonal manner after which the animals and earth are created (*"Let there be"*).

As a woman, you are a special creation because you bear the likeness and image of the King himself. What does that mean? It means two things: we are a *representation* of the King and a *representative* of the King.

A representation of the King

You and I bear the likeness of the King. This means that in our structural capacities (gifts and abilities as humans), we reflect God. We reflect God in our capacity to reason, our will or volition, our capacity to express emotion, and our capacity for intellect – speech, culture, perception and creation of beauty.

In all these areas, we differ from the rest of the King's creation. No other part of creation bears its Creator's likeness in this way. When we use these gifts we are a representation of our King.

But the author of Genesis is careful to include another tidbit of truth. *Gen. 2:7 says, "And the LORD God formed man of the dust of the ground, and breathed into his nostrils the breath of life; and man became a living being."* Despite being *like* God, we are still *distinct* from God.

As Vaughan Roberts aptly says, "Man did not begin as a 'heavenly creature'; he was made of the dust (Heb. `apar) of the ground."[4]

A representative of the King

But there is another aspect of being an image-bearer that we often overlook. God gave us a very important job at the time of creation, a job that he didn't give to any other part of his creation.

Read Genesis 1:28 again.

Mankind is to function as God's representatives over the earth – his sub-regents over creation. God expects us to care for the earth, develop culture, tend to the animals, and to mirror the creativity of the King in doing it!

In fulfilling our role as a sub-regent over the earth, we fully image him – the ultimate creative God who cares for us, who created and sustains the earth, and who cares for all his creation (man, animals, and the earth). When we steward the earth, mankind acts as a representative of God, caring for his creation in his name.

Reviewing Gen. 1 and 2, we see that Adam and Eve had big roles. God tasked Adam with tending and keeping the garden, and God tasked Eve to help Adam do so (Gen. 2:15,18). To both, he gave dominion over the earth and all the animals (Gen. 1:26-28). Some of you are probably worried that I'm about to ask you to start stewarding some plants and animals. If you aren't all that good with plants *or* animals, don't worry, I'm not either. In fact, every pet we've owned has either died or been given away to friends and family.

Today, stewarding the earth looks a little different than in Adam and Eve's day. It is the principle of stewardship that I want you to focus on. To each of his daughters, God has given specific areas of stewardship – and they may or may not include pets. Creatively bearing God's image and stewarding his kingdom can happen in the home, workplace, and community.

Think about some of the ways you might creatively bear God's image as his child and his steward over his kingdom. You can be both a representation and representative of God in caring for your family, in teaching your children to love God's Word, and in serving your neighbors. It takes a creative individual to serve God's kingdom while making copies or coffee at work, just as much as it does to lead out in the boardroom. We are representatives of the King when we serve and obey him in whatever area he has placed us.

And to our work of representing the King there is attached great blessing. We already know that mankind was intended to experience the blessings of God that come from being under God's rule. But we also see specific blessings given to us as we "image God" – as we act as God's steward over creation.

Gen. 1:28 says: *"Then God blessed them, and God said to them, "Be fruitful and multiply; fill the earth and subdue it; have dominion over the fish of the sea, over the birds of the air, and over every living thing that moves on the earth."*

The blessing of being God's sub-regent is tied to man's posterity. Please remember this for later: God ties blessings to man's seed.

So, the image of God, then, is not merely who humanity *is* but also something humanity *does*. We both bear the image of God as a representation of him, but we also 'image' him as his representative here on earth.

CONCLUSION

We see in Gen. 1-2 God's pattern for abundant life: a restful life in his kingdom. To review, we learned that God's kingdom is God's people living in God's place under God's rule and blessing.

When we bear God's image, we are both a representation and representative of the King to his world. As a Daughter of the King, we bear his likeness and act as a sub-regent of his kingdom.

In a world obsessed with titles and positions, the title Daughter of the King is the best, most privileged title we could ever crave. So, why is it we often make much of other labels? In general, we as women love to label ourselves. We love to categories ourselves, others, and our relationships to identify exactly where we fit. We feel most comfortable when we can shape how we view ourselves and how others see us. Check out any social media and you'll see our world is constructed toward labels. We identify ourselves by what we own, what we do, what we say, how we're built, and how we act.

I'm a SAHM (stay-at-home mom) or WAHM (work-at-home mom). I'm a wife. I'm a mama. I'm an executive. I'm a writer. I'm a coffee lover. I'm a thrill seeker. I'm a bookworm.

Recently, an article has been circling my Facebook feed called "23 Signs You're an Introvert." I

have to admit the title caught my eye, because I recently discovered after taking a corporate personality test that I'm part introvert. The news came as quite a surprise to me because for years I've operated under the assumption that I'm an extrovert. I've signed myself up for speaking roles at church. I've pursued large group gatherings over one-on-one discipleship. I've volunteered time and again to be a greeter at Sunday worship services. And perhaps I'm revealing the darkness of my heart, but there was something about the label of an extrovert that I liked. Extroverts are fun to be around. They are often well-liked by their circle of friends.

So, when I discovered that I wasn't as "fun" or "likable" as I thought, I had a five-minute identity crisis. *Maybe I shouldn't volunteer for such public positions,* I thought. *Maybe I'm not gifted to teach. Maybe I should just stay in the background.* Before I knew it, I had completely taken my eyes off the One who has already defined my identity and was searching to better understand myself according to other labels.

Personality tests and even spiritual gift tests can be good things. But when we dwell on man-made labels, we are often guilty of losing our real sense of identity – a Daughter of the King.

The title Daughter of the King is not earned, bargained for, or bestowed because of special giftings or good behavior. It can't be traded in for a seemingly safer label or lost to the super mom next door who grinds her own flour or has spotless floors. The title Daughter of the King can't be tarnished by failure, mistakes, or past regrets. It's an enduring title given to us for no other reason than that we're related to the King. We belong to him, bearing his likeness and his appointment for service in his kingdom.

In your workbook, you have space write out your story as a Daughter of the King. I hope you'll use this tool to follow along and find your place in God's story for the world.

My story:

I am a special creation of God.

You are special for several reasons. First, you were created by the Creator of the universe, and he has declared you a good creation! Even more importantly, the God who worked in your life in the past by creating you is still at work in your life today, even when your circumstances scream otherwise (Rom. 8:28; Phil. 1:6).

Second, you are special because you were created by the Creator of the universe in his own image and likeness. You bear the King's likeness. You are meant to be his special daughter. Second Corinthians 6:18 says, *"I will be a Father to you, and you shall be My sons and daughters, says the Lord Almighty."*

Family ties with our Heavenly Father are crucial for those of us who have lost family members to death or sickness, who are living with broken families, or who have families from which you are separated. You still have a family to which you belong. You belong to God. God created you to be his. You are his - his daughter.

I am meant for something special.

God has a purpose for your life. You were meant to experience a full life of blessing and rest in his kingdom. Matt. 11:28 says, *"Come to Me, all you who labor and are heavy laden, and I will give you rest."* Heb. 4:9-10 echoes this sentiment: *"There remains therefore a rest for the people of God. For he who has entered His rest has himself also ceased from his works as God did from His."*

But God's purpose for us to live in rest doesn't mean we are to be idle. As his daughter, there is much to do. You are meant to serve as his sub-regent over the earth and over his kingdom. You are to use your creativity and status as an image-bearer to bring him glory.

The Bible is God's story, the story of how the King is at work in his kingdom. And as the King's daughter, you play a special part in that story. So, rest assured that God is at work in your life. Even if circumstances seem to scream otherwise, you can be confident that he is at work. In fact, he has given you a special role to play in the King's kingdom.

Chapter 1: The King's Kingdom

1. A story can explain the world and how your life came to be the way it is. Each of us has a story. Describe what your story looks like today. Include any high points, low points, conflicts, and resolution that make your story unique.

2. The Word of God is indeed a lengthy story, comprised of Old and New Testaments and divided by genre – histories, writings and poems, prophecy, letters, etc. What do you believe is the most challenging aspect of connecting all of the different parts of God's story?

3. Is the goal of creation (rest) currently reflected in your life? If so, how? If not, in what areas are you experiencing the most 'unrest'?

4. What are the two ways we image God (reflect the image of God) as stated in the book?

As a Daughter of the King, what are some creative ways you 'image' God (reflect God and act as his sub-regent/servant) in the daily activities you undertake? Think about your unique areas of responsibility (home, office, community). Think about the people God has given you to serve (family, coworkers, church members, neighbors). Think about specific tasks you perform throughout the day.

CHAPTER 2: THE KING'S SUBJECTS REBEL
GENESIS 3

Shortly after I had twins, I realized God had given me a super power. I call this super power Mom-tuition. It's the ability to assess any situation and accurately predict the outcome.

Like when the twins decided that riding a scooter downhill didn't produce nearly the amount of speed they desired. So, they put their little red-heads together and discussed an appropriate course of action. I'm watching all this play out from the patio and my Mom-tuition radar starts blinking softly in my head. I hear them agree that if they can pick up a decent speed with one scooter, image how fast they can go with two scooters! I hold back despite the fact that my internal siren is now screeching. But sure enough, Twin A puts one foot on one scooter and then sets his other foot on the second scooter. There was a split second before I could form the words "No" and the giant push dealt by Twin B. I knew without a shadow of a doubt that this was going to end badly, but I had waited too long to avert the impending disaster.

Mom-tuition. You don't mess around with it. There's a reason God gave us this super power. But even if you don't have children, you might still have this gift. It's the ability to spot a storm brewing on the horizon and know the result will be total destruction.

This gift is both a blessing and a curse, because many times you can avert the result of the storm - or in my case, hair-brained schemes - and limit the damage. But sometimes when you see that storm coming, you know there is absolutely nothing you can do to stop it.

In the previous chapter we learned about God's original pattern for life – that God intended for us to live lives of rest. In fact, Gen. 1-2 shows us

God's pattern for his kingdom – man living at peace with God, with each other, and with the earth. We talked about a definition of kingdom: *God's people in God's place under God's rule and blessing.*

We learned from Gen. 1-2 that Adam and Eve had everything they needed or could ever want; they had a life of rest and purpose. As God's image bearers, they were unique and were given special jobs to care for the garden and serve the King. They lived in his kingdom, under his rule, yet were elevated to a privileged status as his sub-regents. We know that submitting to the King's rule was the way to experience blessing.

But, despite that perfect home, perfect marriage, and perfect relationship with their boss (the King), there was a terrible storm brewing in the garden!

REBELLION IN THE KINGDOM

The law of the kingdom

Now, in the kingdom there was a law. *"And the LORD God commanded the man, saying, "Of every tree of the garden you may freely eat; but of the tree of the knowledge of good and evil you shall not eat, for in the day that you eat of it you shall surely die" (Gen. 2:16-17).* Why did God make this law?

The author is making a very, very important point here, and I don't want you to miss it because we often make Adam's sin about the tree and the forbidden fruit. And while all that is important to the story, it all happens in the following context.

God alone knows what is good for man and what is not good for him.[5] What is best for him and what will be disastrous. In the same way that a master artist owns his artwork, God the Creator is the rightful authority over our lives. He is the infinitely wise Artist, who stands separate from his creation, and the good King who knows what is best for his subjects.

And so, the law of the kingdom is set up to enable man to stay in the kingdom and enjoy and serve the King.

This is our story as Daughters of the King. Our loving King creates us, puts us in a spectacular place just for us, and then gives us the highest position in the entire kingdom. And then on top of all that, the King teaches us how to live at rest and peace.

For us, just like Adam and Eve, God teaches his sub-regents how to experience the good and what will happen if we choose evil. In Gen. 2:17, God tells Adam *"for in the day that you eat of it you shall surely die."*

The law is broken

Read Genesis 3:1-6.

Here we have what history calls "the fall." Adam and Eve chose to break God's commandment. But what was at the heart of the first couple's decision? Scripture is clear that sin was unleashed into humanity at this point. But what is sin and how did it really happen?

I think verse 6 gives us a clue: *"So when the woman saw that the tree was good for food, that it was pleasant to the eyes, and a tree desirable to make one wise, she took of its fruit and ate…."*

Did anything sound familiar to you? The author is pulling our attention to the goodness of creation. Only, instead of God being the one to define the "good," now we see Eve is determining the "good" on her own.

In her estimation, the tree is good because it is good to eat (function), it is good to look upon (appearance), and it is good for wisdom (power).

Now, these things might be true. But do you see the danger? God didn't forbid the couple to eat from the tree for any of these reasons. God put his rule into effect so that man might fully enjoy the "good" God created and be protected from death. God put the rule into effect so that man might have been able to live life at its best – to dwell in the presence of the King, dwell in the King's land, and dwell under the King's rule and benefit from its blessings.

Eve put herself in God's position when she ate the forbidden fruit, acting as the judge of what is "good" and how she would enjoy that "good" apart from God's provision. And as God's sub-regent over his creation, this is the mightiest act of rebellion against the King. The sub-regent is casting off the authority of the King and acting in her own name instead.[6] Ironically, the first couple's quest to determine what constituted both good and evil apart from their King left them unable to enjoy the 'good' at all!

DEFINITION: Sin is any kind of rebellion (in action, attitude, or disposition) against God's moral law and against His holy character (1 John 3:4; Rom. 2:15).

SIGNIFICANCE: Sin corrupts the image of God in us and makes it impossible to obey God perfectly so we may continue to enjoy the blessing of His presence.

CONSEQUENCES OF SIN

Distortion of three major relationships

Read Genesis 3:7-13.

What happens after Adam and Eve break the King's command? Do they die? Not yet, although physically they will eventually taste death. But spiritually, all of the King's warnings come true. The first couple experiences a death in all three major areas of their lives.

1) Man and man – mankind is unable to love others perfectly

Adam and Eve's choice to break the King's commandment meant their relationship with each other became distorted. They no longer lived in harmony with each other. We see this played out immediately after the fall in several ways.

The couple no longer related to each other in intimacy. Sin changed the dynamic of Adam an Eve's relationship. Shame clouded their ability to be truly intimate with each other. Gen. 3:7 speaks of Adam and Eve's new-found shame: *"Then the eyes of both of them were opened, and they knew that they were naked and they sewed fig leaves together and made themselves coverings."* The first couple made a concerted effort to hide from each other, to build layers around those hurts that had sprung up between them.

The couple no longer related to each other in love. Gen. 3:12-13 speaks to self interest: *"Then the man said, 'The woman whom You gave to be with me, she gave me of the tree, and I ate. The woman said, 'The serpent deceived me, and I ate'."*

2) Man and creation – mankind is unable to love God's creation perfectly

Read Genesis 3:16-19.

Not only does sin distort man's relationships with each other, but we also see that sin distorts man's ability to perfectly fulfill his assigned task in the kingdom. Man is no longer able to care and tend the earth in 'rest.' Woman is no longer able to help the man in this task. These tasks still apply, as we'll find out, but they will become extremely difficult.

As a result of Eve's choice to break God's commandment, her assigned task to serve as a helper for her husband would become very difficult (Gen. 3:18).

Her role as *mother* would be characterized by pain. Anyone who has had a child knows the pain of childbirth. Pain characterizes the whole process! The pregnancy, the labor, the birth. For women who are surprised by infertility or childlessness, there is often a silent pain suffered deep within their spirit. God says that the unique area in which Eve is called to serve is going to be difficult—all of it.

Eve's role as *wife* would be characterized by pain as well. Verse 16b says, *"Your desire shall be for your husband and he shall rule over you."* So, what used to be a loving relationship is now described as a painful one. I want to draw your attention to the word "desire" here in verse 16. The same word is used a little later in Gen. 4:6: *"So the LORD said to Cain, 'Why are you angry? And why has your countenance fallen? If you do well, will you not be accepted? And if you do not do well, sin lies at the door. And its <u>desire</u> is for you, but you should rule over it.'*

God was giving Cain a warning against sin. Sin desires mastery over us. Some commentators believe that same sense is used here in Gen. 3. Eve would "desire" her husband in the sense that she would desire to master him. Instead of embracing her role as helper comparable to her husband, Eve would seek to usurp his God-given role as the leader in their relationship (Gen. 2:18). If this interpretation is correct, this marks the origin of the battle of the sexes.

In response to his wife's attempted domination of him, Adam would also tend toward extremes as, dominating her in unloving ways. The text says, *"he shall rule over you"* (Gen. 3:16). The other end of this relational spectrum for Adam would be passivity in his God-ordained role as Eve's protector and provider. Adam would either rule his wife harshly or let her rule him in indifference. The state of many marriages today certainly speaks to the reality of these extremes.

Other commentators believe the word "desire" in Gen. 3:16 should be understood in a more natural sense; Eve would "desire" Adam in ways God did not intend, in an almost idolatrous way. As women, I think we can all relay anecdotal evidence that women often idolize or seek after a man's attention.

In her book, *The Gospel-Centered Woman*, Wendy Aslup says this: "Gen. 3:16 gives us a picture of a woman who looks to the man in her life for emotional and spiritual affirmation and provision in ways that God alone is supposed to provide…The problem for the woman is one of idolatry."[7]

What woman can't attest to either of these struggles – placing too great an emphasis on a man by asking him to fulfill all our needs or placing too little emphasis on a man by nagging, bullying or neglecting his needs? Whichever sense the biblical author intended here, it is clear that marriage – intended as a harmonious relationship – would become a relationship riddled with difficulties. Man and wife would not be able to love each other perfectly.

As a result of Adam's choice to break God's commandment, his assigned task to tend and care for the earth will also be difficult (Gen. 3: 17-19). Just like his wife, his area of service will be characterized by pain, intense effort, and difficulty.

Notice that God didn't take away the privilege of being his sub-regents. As a mother, I am humbled by the grace God demonstrates toward his children in these verses. When my own children refuse to listen to my voice or decide to step outside the bounds I've established for them, I have a tendency to throw in the towel.

How many other mothers have echoed this phrase along with me: *"Just forget it. I'll do it myself!"* Or this one (get ready to wince): *"I can't believe you did that! What were you thinking?"*

It is only by the riches of the King's mercy that he doesn't revoke the roles he designated for his subjects. From this point forward in our personal life stories, the role of the King's sons and daughter will be difficult to fulfill. But, it is still our titled role before our King.

3) Man and God – mankind is unable to love God perfectly

Read Genesis 3:21-23.

First, and most importantly, Adam and Eve's choice to break the King's commandment means they are to be exiled from the kingdom. Not only are they driven from the land, but they are also driven from God's presence. They experience a spiritual death – a separation from God.

Gen. 3:23-24 says: "Therefore the LORD God sent him out of the garden of Eden to till the ground from which he was taken. So He drove out the man; and He placed cherubim at the east of the garden of Eden, and a flaming sword which turned every way, to guard the way to the tree of life."

Could God have allowed Adam and Eve to stay in the garden? Couldn't he have just forgiven them? Or given them a second chance? No. It impossible for a holy God to reside with sinful men. God alone is perfectly holy; he is perfect in his goodness and his power (Ex. 15:11; 1 Sam. 2:2). To be holy means to be separate or set apart. God's perfect 'otherness' means he cannot look on our sin (Is. 59:2; Ps. 66:18). But Scripture also speaks of God's holiness as his moral purity (Is. 6:3; Rev. 4:8). God's holiness means he will always do what is right and always do what it right toward mankind – toward his daughters.

If God allowed sin to persist in his presence, his holiness would have been violated. He would cease to be good. He would cease to be powerful. He would cease to be faithful to his promises. As a result, Adam and Eve were no longer able to experience 'rest' in the garden and dwell in the presence of their King. And because all sin is a violation against God, all sin must be dealt with. It cannot be swept under the rug. The King must act to restore order from chaos and bring justice to evil lest his crown and character be impugned, otherwise the King is not worthy to save.

Can you see how sin tarnishes every area of our life? It tarnishes our relationship with God, our relationship with others (especially our significant others), and our relationship with our assigned tasks. Being a wife, mother, daughter – all these roles are encumbered by sin. Sin makes us unable to fully enjoy the 'good' God intended for us to experience. This passage acknowledges that our life difficulties are real; the Bible speaks to our situation. Sin has tainted the way we live – how we think, how we act, how we feel.

But it hasn't just impacted humanity in an individual sense; sin reaches out and touches all of our major relationships. Sin makes it impossible to love God perfectly, to love each other perfectly, and to love and serve his kingdom perfectly. Sin has touched every aspect of our lives. Rom. 3:23 says, *"…for all have sinned and fall short of the glory of God…"*

No one is immune. It is part of our human nature. Rom. 5:12 says, *"Therefore, just as through one man sin entered the world, and death through sin, and thus death spread to all men, because all sinned - "*

But sin is not the end of our story – or of God's story.

HOPE FROM SIN

The promised Seed

The rest of the biblical story reveals how God is at work to defeat sin and restore his creation – particularly to restore the image of God in man that has been corrupted by sin. We know this because immediately after Adam and Eve sinned, God revealed to them a plan for salvation from sin. The gracious King is at work to save his subjects and restore his kingdom.

Read Genesis 3:15.

God promises the Seed of the woman will conquer the seed of the serpent (evil).

This notion of the Seed of the woman conquering the seed of the serpent (evil) is monumental. The writer does not give us many details. Who is the Seed of the woman? Don't you think Eve wondered that? Here God is giving her a precious promise of salvation that involves her seed – her children.

At the birth of each child, Eve and Adam must have wondered if it would be the promised Seed. And how her hopes must have been utterly dashed when one of her sons (Cain) kills his brother (Abel)! She must have wondered: *What if he was the promised Seed?* Yet, you can see the spark of hope still alive within her as she bore her third son. Gen. 4:24-26 says, *"And Adam knew his wife again, and she bore a son and named him Seth, 'or God has appointed another seed for me instead of Abel, whom Cain killed'."*

Some commentators believe the Seed is representative of the seed of Abraham (Gen. 12). A little later in Genesis, we'll hear about a man named Abraham to whom God promises many sons (seed).

But I believe the writer of Genesis had someone more specific in mind – a male Savior. In fact, many others throughout church history have believed so as well. Between the 3rd and 1st centuries BC, scribes translated the Hebrew Bible into Greek in a book called the Septuagint. Guess how they translated 'seed'? Yep, masculine *and* singular. So, while Gen. 3 does not answer the question "who is the Seed?" the rest of Scriptures will work out this very answer!

Don't forget that word: Seed. We'll be on the lookout for it throughout the rest of our study!

God's protection in the midst of exile

The gracious King did more than just give Adam and Eve a promise. Before their sin required that they be exiled from the King's presence, God provided them clothing for life in their new land. Verse 21 says, *"Also for*

Adam and his wife the LORD God made tunics of skin, and clothed them."

Let's backtrack for a moment. What happened in Gen. 3:7-8? Adam and Eve sewed together fig leaves as a man-made attempt to cover their nakedness. They are trying to hide from God's judgment by hiding their sin. But God still found them, didn't he? Their man-made attempt to cover their nakedness did not work. The biblical author is truly an artist because at this point we see how he is tying it all together. The author is making this important point: Mankind is incapable of covering his own sins; only God can cover our sins.

Some scholars believe this is the first animal sacrifice. If so, we see an early hint at the coming pattern of salvation. We'll discuss this in detail in the coming chapters, so all I really want to emphasize at this point is the King's gracious protection for his vice-regents. They broke his commandment and trust, rebelled against his authority, and tried to usurp his throne as the one to determine the "good" for the kingdom.

And while the King's just and holy nature requires that he cannot leave their sin unpunished (thus they are exiled from the kingdom), he lovingly promises to restore them in time and provides for them even while they live outside his kingdom.

CONCLUSION

At the close of Gen. 3 we are left with both a dismal and hopeful picture of life in the kingdom. We see that man's "happiness does not consist of his being 'like God' so much as it does his being 'with God,' enjoying the blessings of his presence (Ps 16:11)."[8]

Ps. 16:11 says: *"You will show me the path of life; In Your presence is fullness of joy; At Your right hand are pleasures forevermore."*

Isn't that a beautiful reminder for us? As the King, God has the right to determine what is "good" or best for us and how we should enjoy that "good." We are not a law unto ourselves. Our culture prizes autonomy (literally self-law). But Scripture is clear that the path of self-law (autonomy, independence) brings death, disappointment, and pain!

After getting cable for the first time in years, I discovered Bravo TV's "Real Housewives" franchise. It only took one episode to suck me into the over-dramatized world of professionally-applied makeup, hair extensions, lavish parties, and posh apartments. With cameras crammed in their faces, the claims of these so-called housewives are as robust as their shoe collections – wives and mothers who simultaneously want it all, have it all, and control it all.

In the Season 4 title sequence to the Real Housewives of New York City, the cast offered up pithy life philosophies despite the ugly realities often surrounding their daily lives. In her intro spot, cast member LuAnn de Lesseps touted, "I thought I had it good before, but I'm just getting started," referring to her recent transition from Duchess to divorcee. Cast member Sonja Morgan croons in her intro spot, "I have a taste for luxury, and luxury has a taste for me," omitting news she recently filed for bankruptcy.

Despite being educated, beautiful, and cultured, it will come as no surprise that the image of femininity showcased by this reality program runs counter to the portrait of noble women painted on the pages of Scripture. And after watching just a few minutes of the Real Housewives of New York City, I glibly concluded that I wasn't anything like them.

Those women are pernicious, I said to myself. *They are self-absorbed and shallow. They treat their children and husbands poorly. They are territorial and condescending. They don't take responsibility for their actions or words. They play the blame game. They don't view reality in the proper light. Life is all about them.*

As a Christian, work-at-home mother of two, the thick line I drew between us came with great ease. But by the episode's end, I was faced with a rather disarming realization. Could I be more like these "lucky" ladies of reality television than I realized?

And although there are very real and glaring lifestyle differences between us (I don't have live-in help, nannies, or personal assistants, and…oh yeah…I spend most of my day in yoga pants and socks), I couldn't help but wonder if my life unwittingly reflected the culture around me more than my title as a Daughter of the King.

And if my own journey as a woman of God is in danger of poorly reflecting the purposes of my King, then perhaps other Christian women are guilty of conforming their minds to the wrong likeness as well. Here's why I believe it is easier for a modern "church" gal like myself to look more like the housewives of reality television than she realizes.

Very often women buy into the lie that we can have it all – wealth, health, family, career, and the fulfillment of all our personal dreams. And not only has our culture told us that it is possible to *have* it all, but we've also been led to believe that we are *entitled* to it all. Pursuing dreams is not a bad thing. Neither is it bad for a woman to seek to balance career and family in a God-honoring way. But the power of the lie of entitlement resides not simply in the lie itself, but in the doubt such a lie generates in our minds.

In fact, this lie is one of the oldest in the book. Literally. We saw it first appear in the life of the world's very first woman. Even though the good Creator freely gave Eve every good gift for abundant living, she easily bought into the lie that there was something she lacked. Eve discerned that the forbidden fruit was good to eat, "purty" to look at it, and had some great side effects. But it is not the goodness of the fruit that is in dispute. Eve's disobedient actions revealed an ugly doubt in her heart – *if God is withholding good gifts from me, then perhaps He is not such a good God.*

As a testimony to his good character, God had a good plan for Eve's life. But like Eve, women often believe we can and should have all life's good gifts without restriction. A Daughter of the King, however, trusts in the good character of her King as the sole giver of good gifts.

More often, however, Christian women buy into the lie that we know best. With the woman as the ultimate authority in her own life, she then becomes the executive determiner of what's best for her. Like Eve, Daughters of the King are often deceived into doubting not only the good character of our King, but the good directives of our King as well.

Still today, we often operate under the deception that we can enjoy the goodness of life apart from the good Creator himself. As New York Housewife Cindy Barshop says in her Season 4 intro spot, *"I have all I ever wanted, and it's all on my own terms."* While we might not resort to the wild shenanigans of reality TV stars, hijacking the train can be accomplished in subtle ways in the life of Christian women. If married, we can easily disregard God's good Word in the Scriptures regarding the roles of husband and wife (Eph. 5:22-23). If single, we can easily disregard God's good Word concerning the joy of sex within the parameters of the marriage relationship (1 Cor. 7:2). If leaders in the church, we can easily disregard God's good Word for women in ministry (1 Tim. 2:12). All are good gifts – marriage, sex, ministry – but their goodness is to be enjoyed in the way our good God designed.

Furthermore, not every good gift is good for every woman. Daughters of the King trust that a good King gives good gifts in accordance with his good knowledge for our good purpose.

The lives of the Real Housewives warn us that sin results in, at best, bad marriages, divorce, bankruptcy, or participating in a really bad music video at the age of 45. But at its worst, sin propels us on a track of desperation and destruction.

Mom-tuition. It's the ability to assess any situation and accurately predict the outcome. This super-power aided me much while watching the Real Housewives. But this skill comes less from motherhood and more from the Spirit as he illuminates his Word in my life. And reality-shows aside, it's a skill that helps me evaluate where the train of my own life is dangerously veering off track.

My Story:

I am a Daughter of the King.

We've seen that life in God's kingdom was designed to be the best kind of life. Living with God in God's place and under God's rule is the path of blessing. But we often think we know better or that we can somehow craft a plan that is superior to his. Let's not continually repeat the sin of Eve over and over again. We are not a law unto ourselves. We are Daughters of the King, intended to live a life of rest with the King in his kingdom.

I was created for a special purpose.

As you set about your daily tasks – grocery store runs, chauffeuring children from events and school, receiving dark news about family, or taking an unexpected financial hit - remember that our King is good! Just as he protected and promised salvation to Adam and Eve, we can trust him with our lives. With everything. Specifically, we must trust God to determine the good in life for us, and then trust that the "good" plan he has for us, truly IS good even when our circumstances scream otherwise.

"You will show me the path of life; In Your presence is fullness of joy; At Your right hand are pleasures forevermore." Ps. 16:11

Chapter 2: The King's Subjects Rebel

1. In the space below, write out the three-part definition of the kingdom used in the book (taken from Vaughan Roberts's book *God's Big Picture*).

2. Describe Eve's decision to disobey the King's command in Gen. 3:6. Ultimately, what was Eve saying about herself and God when she

broke God's Law? In what ways do you seek to cast off God's authority as the one to determine what is "good" in life?

3. What does sin do to the image of God in mankind? (Hint: the answer can be found in the definition of sin).

4. What are the three major relationships distorted by sin in Gen. 3:7-23? How does sin distort each of them? Think of an area of life in which you are currently experiencing conflict. How is sin at play?

What specific hope does God give his daughters in Gen. 3:15 for restoring the image of God within us?

CHAPTER 3: THE KING'S PROMISE
GENESIS 4-49

My friend Nivedita (I call her Nive) grew up Hindu in northern India. Her hardworking parents provided her with every opportunity they could afford, even enrolling her in a Christian high school. Yet, Nive always knew she would leave home someday. Despite coming from a loving, stable family, she always knew she had a different purpose. Like a small-town girl working diligently to move to the big city, Nive believed higher education was her ticket to finding a life apart from the reality experienced by many of the women of her homeland.

So, with a civil engineering degree under her belt and self-taught computer programming skills, Nive left the familiar behind and moved across the ocean to foreign place. She knew no one and very little of her new home, the U.S. So, she was caught off guard when she met someone for the first time in her life: the King.

A few years after moving to the U.S., Nive met and married her husband, Randy, who led her to Christ. But a classic analyst at heart, Nive's surrender to faith was hard-won. Like many of us, Nive had many false beliefs to weed out and filter through the spectrum of God's Word. But it has been one of the most immense joys of my life to watch her wrestle with the Scriptures and apply them to her life without damaging the Christ-honoring part of her lovely culture.

I think, above all, Nive will tell you that faith was the biggest leap she ever took, even more so than moving to a foreign land and leaving behind her loved ones, her comforts, and all things familiar. Like any Daughter of the King, Nive's journey of faith was not without its bumps. Yet, as we'll see in the remainder of the book of Genesis, being a Daughter of the King means trusting in the eternal promises of God.

So far our tour of the biblical story has occurred at a leisurely pace. Our tour vehicle has taken us through the lush Garden of Eden to view all its beauty and the goodness of God's kingdom.

Do you remember the definition of God's kingdom? God's people in God's place under God's rule and blessing.

We stopped by the tree of the knowledge of good and evil to observe the consequences of sin in God's kingdom. Specifically, sin required God's people be removed from his holy presence, making it impossible for them to dwell together and enjoy the blessings of his rule: rest.

In this chapter, we're going to pick up some speed. Our little tour vehicle is going to fly through the rest of Genesis. But remember we are still on the lookout for something: God's promise concerning Eve's Seed and what that coming Seed means for the King's kingdom.

THE PROMISES OF GOD

Time has passed since God gave his first clue to the hope of salvation in Gen. 3:15. Many generations have arisen from Adam and Eve, but God chose to wait until one man was born through which to reveal his specific purposes for the coming Seed: Abraham.

Read Genesis 12:1-9.

God made a promise to Abraham. That promise had three components:

God's people – God promised Abraham that his line of descendants will become a great nation, God's people. (Gen. 12:2 - "I will make you a great nation.")

God's place – God promised Abraham that his descendants will be given land in which to dwell. (Gen. 12:1 – "to a land I will show you" and Gen. 12:2 – 'nation' implies territory.)

God's rule and blessing – God promises Abraham that his descendants will receive blessings as they live as his people. These blessings would trickle down to all other nations. (Gen. 12:2- "I will bless you" and "you shall be a blessing," and in Gen. 12:3 – "in you all the families of the earth shall be blessed.")

Did you notice that the promises God makes to Abraham fit with our definition of the kingdom? God's people in God's place under God's rule and blessing. Let's take a closer look at these promises made to Abraham.

God's People

God promises that he will make Abraham the beginning of a great nation – not just numerically speaking, but a nation that would be set apart for God.

In Gen. 12:7, can you guess what word God used for "descendants?" He used the term '*zera* or seed. Remember, we said this was a very important word – a word rich with covenant promises. We first encountered it in Gen. 3:15. God promises to send a Seed (a man) to defeat sin. And so, Abraham must know that God's promise to increase his seed must mean more than becoming a great nation. Abraham's seed would be the line through which salvation would come.

God's Place

Second, God promises to give Abraham land. This is not just a gift of prime real estate; this land would be the location for the future fulfillment of all God's promises to Abraham. Much hinged on acquiring this land.

But, in order to dwell in the Promised Land with God, Abraham was required first to forsake his homeland, his family, and his past. He could not dwell with God in his own existing country. And so Abraham, acting in faith, left the familiar behind in order to dwell with God (Gen. 12:1, 4-8).

God's Rule and Blessing

God's third promise to Abraham was that he and his descendants would receive great blessings and protection and that through them all other nations would be blessed. So, from the very beginning we see God's intention to restore the whole world – all nations – from the effects of sin.

However, God still had a specific manner in which this plan to restore the world would occur, and that plan used one people, one nation through which to mediate his salvation. Abraham and his descendants (his seed) would stand as an example of what life in God's kingdom should look like. God intended for Abraham and his descendants (later, Israel) to stand as an example of God's people, living in God's place (the Promised Land), and under God's rule. And when they fulfilled this calling, they would be the recipients of great blessings.

THE COVENANT OF GOD

After God had given these promises to Abraham, Scripture says Abraham believed God and God "credited it to him as righteousness" (Gen. 15:6).

Read Genesis 15:1-8; 18.

What is a covenant?

Definition: Covenant – is a binding, permanent relationship, solemnly agreed to by two parties and ratified by a sign.

Significance: God relates to man through his covenant. He gives his people an **unconditional** promise of protection and provision, expecting them "to make their own promises to obey him."[9]

There are a couple of characteristics of God's covenant with man that I think we should note because we often think of a covenant as a promise. God's covenant with his people is much weightier than a promise. Likewise, we often think of a covenant like a marriage contract – an agreement between two parties that can be dissolved if one of the parties fails to uphold their obligations. But the covenant between God and man is different: it is permanent.

The covenant between God and man is based not on two equal parties; rather, the covenant between God and man is based on God's ability and character to fulfill his promises as the stronger party.

However, this does not mean man has no responsibilities in the covenant relationship. In fact, it is quite the opposite. Man is obligated to be loyal to the covenant and obey his King. So, while the covenant relationship is unconditional, the *blessings* of the covenant with Abraham are *conditional*.[10]

If man obeys the King, he will receive blessings. If man disobeys the King, he will receive curses. In short, God would fulfill all his covenant promises to Abraham, despite disobedience (cf. Gen. 15: 12-16).

When I taught this study to my home church in San Antonio, I used a hand motion to bring this concept to life. First, make two fists. Second, put one fist on top of the other. The top fist represents God; the bottom fist represents man. When man disobeys the King, he is no longer in alignment in his covenant relationship (move your bottom fist from under your top fist). So, even though the King remains the same in his intentions and love, it is man who is no longer in the King's presence and enjoying the blessings of his rule. But when man does obey the King (move your fist back to its original position under the top fist), the blessings of being in the presence of the King flow freely. The important element is that the King in unswerving in his commitment to his covenant.

In telling you about the mechanics of covenants, I'm not just giving you facts. We are laying the foundation for understanding how God relates to man. God covenants with his people to provide for them based on his character and his ability. It has nothing to do with our abilities.

God is faithful to his covenant promises. And while we are expected to be loyal to God and be obedient to him, our failures do not nullify his covenant relationship with us. We would identify that as a very New Testament concept, indeed. And we'll be sure to revisit this topic later in our study.

An Eternal Relationship

And so we see several key things about the covenant made with Abraham, namely it was a very special relationship:

An eternal covenant

God's covenant was not made with Abraham and his immediate seed – but all those from Abraham's line, forever!

Read Genesis 17:1-2, 6-8.

For the Jews reading this passage later, this promise was crucial to their understanding of the covenant. Remember, the head of the race (Adam) was kicked out of the garden. He was exiled from his land, where he walked with God and dwelt with God in rest. Outside of Eden, the first couple was separated from God and lived lives characterized by pain, hard work, fighting, and death.

So, the Jews reading Genesis 17 would have known that the promise of land, as an eternal inheritance, signified a promise to once more dwell in a specific place with God and to dwell in rest with him.

A royal covenant

From Abraham a royal line would come. This adds another shade of meaning to the promise of salvation through the coming Seed. The Seed of the covenant would come from a line of kings. Verse 6 says, *"I will make you very fruitful; I will make nations of you, and kings will come from you."*

And these kings would come from the offspring of Abraham and Sarah (Gen. 17:15-16). And these kings would come from the line of Isaac (Gen. 17:19-21).

Covenant Obligations

So, we've already learned that God's covenant with his people was unconditional. He would remain faithful to fulfill his covenant promises to Abraham's seed. But we've also learned that covenants carried with them obligations. The weaker party was obligated to remain loyal. Therefore, we see that God asked Abraham to "be blameless" (Gen. 17:1). God didn't expect Abraham to be perfect. However, God did require Abraham to obey his Word – his rule – in the same way he required Adam to obey his rule in the garden.

Read Genesis 22:1-19.

The difficulty of obedience cannot be overemphasized here. Can you imagine the horror that Abraham and Sarah must have felt when God asked them to sacrifice their only son to him? To sacrifice your loved one is reprehensible enough, but they had been specifically promised in Gen. 15 that the royal Seed would come from Isaac's line. Both of them must have feared – in their old age – that Isaac might be their only chance to see God's promises come true. Sarah probably thought she would never have another son!

God required a sacrifice from Abraham – specifically a burnt offering. We'll learn more about these sacrifices and how they figured into the covenant, but let's just say at this point that a sacrifice was required.

But more importantly, we know that it was God that provided the sacrifice, and Abraham had faith that God would provide it (Gen. 22:8). In verse 13, the provision is made. Gen. 22:13 says, *"Then Abraham lifted his eyes and looked, and there behind him was a ram caught in a thicket by its horns. So Abraham went and took the ram, and offered it up for a burnt offering instead of his son. And Abraham called the name of the place, The-LORD-Will-Provide; as it is said to this day, "In the Mount of the LORD it shall be provided."*

Only God can cover our sins. Remember Adam and Eve's man-made attempt to cover their own sin? Did it work? No. Only the coverings provided by God were and are adequate. The same picture is painted for us here in Gen. 22. Man's sacrifices are not enough to cover their sin. Only the sacrifices provided by God are adequate.

God provided the sacrifice. Here we see the pattern for salvation – salvation by substitution. We'll talk more about this in the coming chapters, but I want to mention it at this point. It is crucial to see that salvation came to the patriarchs through their covenant relationship with God – God provided their salvation based on their faith.

In Gen. 15:6, the author of Genesis said this about Abraham: *"And he believed in the Lord, and He accounted it to him for righteousness."*

God's vehicle for salvation has always been faith. It is the same today, just like in Abraham's day.

In Eph. 2:8-9, Paul says, *"For by grace you have been saved through faith, and that not of yourselves; it is the gift of God, not of works, lest anyone should boast."* God determines the way he will be worshipped. When we make our worship about our offerings, our gifts, our service, our traditions, we are making salvation about something other than faith. Just like Abraham, we must place our trust in God to provide a suitable sacrifice on our behalf.

CONCLUSION

The rest of Genesis recounts the story of Abraham's line and the state of the covenant. Sometimes Abraham's descendants get it right. Other times they fail miserably. There are dozens of near misses in Genesis where the reader cannot help but wonder how God will be able to fulfill his covenant promises in light of sin and sinful people.

But by the time we come to the close of Genesis, we see Abraham's line had grown into to an entire nation. His son Isaac bore a son named Jacob. And from Jacob, would come the 12 tribes of Israel.

At the end of Genesis, we see Jacob is at the end of his life, and from his deathbed he issues last words concerning the "last days" to each of his sons. Gen. 49:10 says, *"The scepter shall not depart from Judah, nor a lawgiver from between his feet, until Shiloh comes; and to Him shall be the obedience of the people."*

Jacob is making an important prophecy: from the line of Judah a figure would come carrying a royal scepter and before whom people would bow in obedience. This figure would be authoritative, law-giving, and royal. Who is this kingly figure? Jacob doesn't mention names. But for the rest of the biblical story, we will watch the tribe of Judah with interest, knowing that it is through the lineage of this tribe that we can expect to see all God's promises to Abraham and Sarah fulfilled.

And from Abraham onward, the story of Scripture anticipates a man with a royal heritage through which the original kingdom may be restored. In the coming chapters we will be given additional clues as to the identity of this kingly figure.

My Story:

My covenant with the King is permanent and eternal, despite my own failures.

The story of Scripture explains why our lives are often broken, a wreck, and full of pain and suffering. Sin has messed everything up. Most importantly, it has separated us from our King and expelled us from his peaceful perfect kingdom of rest.

On our own, we will never be perfect enough to dwell with a holy God or get back into the kingdom. But good news surfaces later in the biblical story. God has made a way, despite our failures, for us to dwell with him. This was his promise to Abraham, and this is his promise to his daughters today. The God who makes these promises is faithful into eternity. And while we are still expected to be loyal and obedient to him, our failures do not nullify his covenant relationship with us.

The King's daughters, those who have put their faith in his promises, cannot be separated from him. Paul tells us so in Rom. 5:38-39: *"For I am persuaded that neither death nor life, nor angels nor principalities nor powers, nor things present nor things to come, nor height nor depth, nor any other created thing, shall be able to separate us from the love of God which is in Christ Jesus our Lord."*

But above all, we cannot be loyal to a King we've never met. Have you entered into a covenant relationship with the King? In the coming chapters, we'll talk more about how that covenant applies to us.

My worship of the King occurs on his terms, not mine.

The book of Genesis stands as both a hope and a warning: we cannot worship God on our own terms. God determines the manner in which he will be worshiped, and he requires worship characterized by faith.

In most cultures, there is a specific day set aside to worship. During this special time, people either worship the real King or the king they've constructed - sports on Sunday, shopping on Saturday, sleeping in on the weekends, going out with the girls to get a break from the workweek. These western gods are every bit as real as false idols in India, China, or other distant lands circling the globe. It doesn't matter if they are wooden statues to which incense is burned or seemingly good desires that have captured our heart over our King.

Even for those of us who live in light of the real King, there is always a tendency to make our worship about the work of our hands. It is much easier to make worship about the things we've done - how many times we've volunteered to serve, how early we arrive to help set up at church, how much money we've given and to whom, what temptations we successfully avoided - rather than surrendering our whole heart to the King. Driven by pride, this type of worship dethrones the King and enthrones 'self' in his place. This is not the type of worship outlined by the King, even if it happens in the context of a church or the name of religion. God doesn't share his throne. He alone is King.

The King only enters into a covenant relationship with those who demonstrate faith in his promises. But here's the good news, once we have entered into that relationship of faith with him, we eternally and permanently dwell with him in a forever home.

Regardless of home or country, the King will always seek out and find his daughters. Just as he did for Abraham, God beckons women with no family and gives them a place to belong. He calls women from broken homes and gives them an eternal dwelling. And sometimes he asks us to do hard things, like my friend Nive, and leave behind the familiar and the comfortable so that he could invite her to his kingdom as his daughter.

Nive's position as a Daughter of the King has turned her into a missionary of sorts, particularly because she seeks to see her parents, brother, and four sisters become sons and daughters of the King one day. The thought of her family experiencing life under God's rule and blessing constantly feed her thoughts and prayers. Just as Nive misses her family across the sea, so our Heavenly Father yearns to bring his family together from around the world – all his sons and daughters. And for all those who enter into his covenant, the King promises to do so.

Chapter 3: The King's Promise

1. In Gen. 12:1-9, God made a three-part promise to Abraham. Identify

the three components. For extra points, describe how God's promises to Abraham line up with the definition of God's kingdom (God's people, in God's place, under God's rule and blessing).

2. Describe God's covenant with man. What is it? Who is the responsible party? Is it conditional or unconditional? What obligations came with it?

3. Consider this statement: God's vehicle for salvation has always been faith. How is faith the same today as it was in Abraham's day? (Hint: think 'promises')

4. In Gen. 49, who is the object of God's promise? What terms are used to describe him?

Review the "my story" section of this chapter. How would you describe your relationship with God? Is it based on what *you* do or what God has done and promises to do in your life? In forming your answer, consider where you spend the bulk of time, money, commitments, and emotional energy.

CHAPTER 4: THE KING'S GRACE
EXODUS – DEUTERONOMY

Have you ever broken something and then tried to glue it back together?

On a trip to China, I returned home with a miniature clay teapot. Hands down, it was probably my favorite souvenir from my trip. It wasn't expensive, in fact it only cost a few dollars, but it was beautiful and delicate. You could tell it had been made by a master craftsman, so I kept it on a high shelf out of reach of little hands.

But I didn't just put the teapot on display. I used it to make steaming cups of fragrant oolong tea. In fact the more I used it, the more fragrant my tea became because the walls of the dark clay absorbed the aroma of the tea leaves. But even more than its beauty or function, the little teapot had sentimental value to me. It was valuable because of what it represented – a time when my husband and I were traveling and meeting new friends and experiencing the adventures that come with being immersed in new cultures. My little teapot was a storehouse of memories.

A few years ago, I walked into my home office just in time to watch a set of chubby little hands reach up to grab it. In slow motion, I watched as my little teapot tumbled from its spot on the bookshelf onto the wood floor where it cracked and shattered into what seemed like a million splinters.

As I was sweeping up the pieces, I felt like I was picking up little pieces of my heart! Because I knew that once something is broken, even if repaired, it never quite looks the same...or functions the same.

As Daughters of the King, we often look more like broken teapots than lovely vessels. Busted and broken by marriage or failed relationships, we wear the everyday cracks and chips from life in visible ways. We can also bear those pains silently, too. Thankfully, it is broken vessels that the King enjoys using the most through which to demonstrate his all-surpassing power (2 Cor. 4:7). This is certainly true for all God's people – particularly Israel.

In this chapter, our story takes us through the rest of the Law (the first five books of the Old Testament). It is the story of God's covenant with Israel as it begins to grow into a nation. We already know that man's relationship with God had been shattered, much like my little teapot. Once sin entered the world, life never looked the same or functioned the same. All of life was in need of, not just repair, but a miraculous restoration.

GOD'S GRACE IN SALVATION

God saves His people through substitutionary atonement

As we peer into this part of the biblical story, we find Israel in a very terrible spot. Abraham's descendants were promised land, but instead they found themselves in slavery to Egypt. They had been promised to be God's people under his rule, but instead they find themselves in a harsh existence serving ruthless men. This type of life is a far cry from the restful service God envisioned for his obedient servants in the land of Eden. Their lives were broken and didn't look or function the same.

But we see God is always at work, and so he chooses a man named Moses to head up a task force to free the King's subjects.

Read Exodus 12:1-13.

Again, we see God at work laying the pattern for salvation – salvation that occurs by substitution. That night, the Lord kills the firstborn of all the Egyptians, while sparing the sons of Israel. This may sound dreadful, but remember God always provides a substitute – a means of escaping our judgment. These means are on his terms, not our own. As such, the Israelites were to sprinkle the blood of a lamb on their door posts. The Lord said he would pass over those houses marked by the blood of the lamb leaving them unharmed.

Sprinkling their door with the blood of a lamb was a mighty act of faith. The Israelites were taking God at his word and trusting him to save them. They were obedient to worship God in the way God prescribed. Had the Israelites chosen not to do so, their first born would have most certainly died as well. All men are under God's judgment due to sin.

But instead, a substitution takes place: God allowed the death of an innocent lamb to act as a substitute for the death of Israel's first born. Again, it wasn't the magic blood of the lamb that saved the first born of the Israelites. Rather, the blood was a statement of their faith in God and an acknowledgement that they too deserved to die. Old Testament scholar John Sailhamer says this was "obedience to the Word of the Lord," and "evidence of their faith and trust in him."[11]

In this first Passover event, we see a vivid picture and reason for the sacrificial system used in the Old Testament. The sacrificial system enabled some measure of relationship. A holy God cannot dwell with unholy people. At least, he cannot without ceasing to be holy. So, as a measure of God's grace, he institutes a sacrificial system.

Definition: **Sacrifice** – "the physical elements a worshiper brings to God to express devotion, thanksgiving, or the need for forgiveness."[12]

Significance: Sacrifices enabled a holy God to dwell with unholy people. The sacrificial system partially restores God's relationship with His people.

It is important to note that the sacrifices themselves did not save the people – the people are saved through faith as Scripture attests (Heb. 10:1-4). Rather, for man, the sacrifice is a physical act of acknowledgment of sin and the need for forgiveness. And for God, the sacrifice fulfills the consequence of a blood sacrifice (death) for sin (cf. Gen. 3; Lev. 17:11). The result of the sacrifice is "God has dealt with sin and can continue to live with the Israelites."[13]

The people were given specific requirements for offering a sacrifice to the Lord. They did not offer sacrifices as they saw fit, but according to specific instructions from God. The people were to offer daily sacrifices as well as an annual sacrifice – offered on the Day of Atonement (Yom Kippur) by the High Priest. It is this Day of Atonement to which I want us to pay particular attention.

Read Leviticus 16:5-10, 20-22.

Again, we see the pattern of substitutionary atonement. On the Day of Atonement, the High Priest is required to sacrifice two goats on behalf of the people. The first is killed as an offering for sin. Over the head of the second goat, the High Priest confesses the sins of all the people and then the goat is led away alive and released into the wilderness (Lev. 16:21-22).

The pattern of substitutionary atonement removes both the penalty of sin (death) and the guilt it leaves behind. Only God can remedy our sin. We must accept His perfect sacrifice – the perfect substitution. And when God remedies our sin, he removes all guilt – the picture of a goat being led away into an uninhabited place.[14]

And so, while sacrifices in themselves did not provide salvation, they did enable some measure of relationship between man and God, however imperfectly. Although the sacrificial system was intended as a measure of God's grace to restore some form of relation with His people, it did not permanently take away the people's sin. The people needed to offer sacrifices for as long as they continued to sin. So, you can see the problem. The restoration of the relationship between God and man is not complete, it is not restored to the same level of intimacy that Adam and Eve experienced in the garden with God. So, already the biblical author is setting us up to anticipate a better, permanent, lasting sacrifice.

GOD'S GRACE IN THE LAW

We've already seen that it is through God's grace in the sacrificial system of substitution, that the relationship between God and man is partially restored. But during this time period, we also see another measure of God's grace given to the Israelites: the Law.

Read Exodus 19:1-6; 20:1-17.

Sometimes we mistakenly take the Law as a precondition for salvation – as if one is saved by adherence to the Law. But God's covenant with his people was unconditional and based on faith. This is important because it is tempting to believe that the Old Testament teaches a works-oriented salvation, but that is simply not the case. Scripture is clear the only way to enter into a relationship with God is through faith.

As Vaughan Roberts says, "But if obedience to the law is not the path to membership in the covenant people of God, it is required for the enjoyment of blessing within the covenant."[15]

God says as much in Ex. 19:5: "*Now therefore, if you will indeed obey My voice and keep My covenant, then you shall be a special treasure to Me above all people; for all the earth is Mine."*

Israel was expected to be loyal to their covenant relationship, and they demonstrated their loyalty through obedience to the Law. As the people lived under the King's rule and obeyed his commandments, they would receive great blessings. Therefore, the Law enables a partial restoration of the blessings of the covenant to the people.

In the Law, we see a partial fulfillment of that Abrahamic promise of great blessings. Ex. 19:4 reveals that as God's covenant people, the Israelites were to act as his co-rulers on the earth; specifically they were to be a kingdom of priests. Ex. 19:4-6 says, *"You have seen what I did to the Egyptians, and how I bore you on eagles' wings and brought you to Myself. Now therefore, if you will indeed obey My voice and keep My covenant, then you shall be a special treasure to Me above all people; for all the earth is Mine. And you shall be to Me a <u>kingdom of priests and a holy nation.</u>"*

The Law testifies that obedience brings blessings, but it does not bring salvation. And the people can only experience these blessings of being the King's sub-regents when they are living holy lives (as defined by the Law) (cf. Deut. 26:18-19). The Law was intended to be the means by which God's people were brought back under the King's rule so that they might enjoy his blessings and be a blessing to other nations.

Yet the New Testament is clear. While the Law restored blessings to God's covenant people, it did so imperfectly (John 1:16-17). God's sub-regents were still sinners, and throughout the Old Testament we see Israel struggling to obey. As such, they forfeited many of God's blessings. And so again, the reader is set up to anticipate a greater restoration of the blessings God's people might experience under God's rule.

GOD'S GRACE IN THE TABERNACLE

Along with the sacrificial system and the Law, God added a third measure of grace to his people – his tabernacle. As the Jews wandered in the wilderness, the tabernacle acted as a portable temple where they worshiped and offered sacrifices.

Read Exodus 25:8-9.

When we look back to the original kingdom in Eden, we see the King dwelt directly with man. They walked together and spent time talking together. But with the entrance of sin, what happened? Adam and Eve were exiled from the kingdom and put out of the presence of the Lord.

The Promised Land, then, was intended to be a place where God and man could reside together once again. But even before the Israelites arrive in the Promised Land, God gave them a measure of grace in the tabernacle.

The tabernacle was to be a dwelling place for God. In fact, the word tabernacle comes from the word "to dwell."[16] But the tabernacle was also a place for God to meet with man. Therefore, in some translations you see the description "tabernacle of meeting" used (See Ex. 25:8-9, 22; 40:34-38). Above all, the tabernacle would become the centerpiece of worship for the Jews.

When the Jews finally entered the Promised Land and built a permanent temple in which they dwelt with the Lord, it was still not a perfect restoration of the pattern of life experienced by Adam and Eve in the garden. Like my little teapot that I tried to glue back together, life just wasn't as beautiful or functional as it once was. God could dwell with man in the temple, but it was not the intimate dwelling that occurred between God and man when they walked together in the garden.

In the tabernacle/temple, only the High Priest was allowed to enter the specific space inhabited by the presence of the Lord – the Holy of Holies. And even then, the High Priest could only enter one day a year, on the Day of Atonement, to offer a sacrifice on behalf of all the people.

Even the measure of grace offered in the tabernacle pointed to the need for a better temple, a better tabernacle, a better place wherein God and man could dwell more intimately together. Their relationship had been partially restored - but it was not complete. There were still gaping cracks and missing pieces.

CONCLUSION

God is a gracious God. His dealings with his people, Israel, proved this. He extended three measures of grace all purposed to restore the relationship between God and man.

Through the sacrificial system, *the covenant status of being God's people* is partially restored.

Through the law, *the covenant blessings that stem from the God's rule* are partially restored.

Through the tabernacle, *the covenant promise of dwelling with God in a specific place* is partially restored.

But the Old Testament Jews knew the provision of God's grace in this era were not the ultimate fulfillment of the promises made to Abraham. Throughout the rest of the Pentateuch, we see God's people desperate and longing for a better life.

They longed for a better *sacrifice* that permanently covered their sin. They longed for a better *way of life* than the blessings procured by the Law. They longed for a better *temple* in which to more intimately dwell with God.

And above all, they constantly longed for that coming Seed – the King from the tribe of Judah – whose reign would completely and totally fulfill all these promises of God's people living in God's place and experiencing the blessings of God's rule (Gen. 3:15; 49). They knew this coming Seed would usher in the permanent restoration of the kingdom of God.

As we opened this chapter, I told you about my broken teapot. In order for my teapot to be as beautiful as it once was and hold water as well as it used to, it needs to be more than just repaired. It needs a total restoration. Tape and super glue cannot undo the damage that was done; they are temporary fixes to a fundamentally rooted problem.

In the same way, our relationship to the King will never look as lovely or function as well without total and complete restoration. We are, after all, completely and totally, broken.

You might feel that way today, shattered and beyond repair. You might be painfully aware that the way you are trying to pick up all the pieces and hold them together just isn't going to work. You know that all it will take is one more discouraging word or one more financial setback before all the pieces come crashing down around you. You can't hold on by yourself forever, and you weren't meant to.

I never threw that little teapot away. I taped it back together, or at least I tried. In the middle of the teapot, there is a gaping hole where one giant chunk of clay is still missing. But I kept the teapot, because it is a graphic reminder to me of my relationship with my King. In fact, I keep it tucked away on a shelf as though it is still a valuable and priceless artifact. My little broken teapot reminds me, above all else, that God loves me, his daughter, as a chipped vessel. And every time I see it, it whispers to my heart that it took a movement of grace, a miraculous intervention, for me to become a Daughter of the King. Thankfully, our King is capable of such things.

Do you need a miraculous restoration, too?

My Story:

Only God can repair and restore me.

Only God can remedy our sin. Just as my little teapot could never hope to grow arms and conduct a repair on itself, our restoration as Daughters of the King can come by the hands of the King himself. The King remedies our sin by being the perfect sacrifice, the perfect substitution for the penalty of death that was and is marked for us. And when we decide to surrender to the King's rule, we find life abundant. We are transformed, changing from broken by sin to a Daughter of the King.

Chapter 4: The King's Grace

1. What was the purpose of the sacrificial system in the King's kingdom? If animal sacrifices did not save God's people, then why were they offered?

2. What was the purpose of the Law in the King's kingdom? If adherence to the Law did not save God's people, then why was it given?

3. What did the tabernacle (and later the temple) represent in the King's kingdom?

4. Do you agree with the assessment that the Law, the sacrificial system, and the tabernacle were gifts of God's grace? If not, please share why. If so, please share how these three ways of relating to God were demonstrations of grace.

Reading through the Law fills me with gratitude that the King has made a better, fuller gift of grace available to his daughters! Describe the time you accepted the King's gift of grace in your life. Share how the King has repaired and restored you even as you await the final chapter in your story.

CHAPTER 5: THE KING'S SUBJECTS DEMAND A KING
JOSHUA – ESTHER

As infants my twin boys loved to throw food over their high chairs to our eager puppy waiting below with baited breath.

They knew the word 'no.' They also knew that if they disregarded the word 'no,' there would be consequences. But as soon as the consequences were doled out, they would turn and do it again.

I always hoped my children would grow out of that phase. But you know what? Even at age 5, they still walk in the same pattern, it doesn't matter if it's hitting, name calling, or disrespectful language. We say 'no.' They disobey. There are consequences – sometimes painful, sometimes not, but always memorable. And then, we rinse and repeat. What mom isn't familiar with this story?

But forget about the consequences for a minute. Our choices reveal something about ourselves: they reveal the *real* state of our heart – where our loyalty lies. When my boys disobeyed and continued to throw food over their high chairs, they were communicating to us the contents of their hearts. They do not want to be ruled by me or my husband. They want to rule themselves.

But this reality isn't true of just kids; it's true of adults as well. We make terrible choices knowing that they will only reap pain. Our choices reveal much more than foolish thinking, immature reactions, or inadvertent mistakes. Our choices reveal something about the loyalty of our hearts. Disobedience isn't a phase we grow out of; disobedience is a pattern from which we must be rescued.

I have a dear sister in Christ who knows the pain of this self-induced cycle of a wayward heart. After one failed marriage, she jumped into another relationship she knew to be doomed from the start. In each of these relationships she was looking for something that she would not and did not find in her partner – the love of her King. And in the end, those wayward relationships had eroded little parts of her life that were intended to be showpieces of God's kingdom. Her choices had impacted her career, her home, her friendships, and her walk with the King.

Sometimes, as the King's daughters, we seek affection and affirmation from outside the throne room. And despite knowing the consequences of a wandering heart, we chose to travel down a road we know only leads to destruction. Not too long ago, my King rescued my friend again. When I saw her recently I noticed how her spiritual transformation reflected on her countenance. The King had elevated her from embarrassed to joyful and from burnt out to overflowing with gratitude. She never looked better; she looked restful. And I rejoiced knowing that it is not the pattern of poor choices that define us; it is our relationship to the King that does.

In this chapter we are going to take a birds-eye look at the nation of Israel spanning the **History Books** of the Bible (Joshua through Esther). While we won't study every book in this section, I want you to pay careful attention to how Israel's patterned choices of sin led them to experience inevitable consequences and what their disobedience revealed about their hearts.

The book of **Joshua** begins as Israel is poised to finally enter the Promised Land. Joshua is chosen by Moses as the leader of the nation, and he leads God's people to overtake the land's inhabitants and claim God's promise of a land under God's rule. And they succeed.

Josh. 21:43-45 says, *"So the LORD gave to Israel all the land of which He had sworn to give to their fathers, and they took possession of it and dwelt in it. The LORD gave them rest all around, according to all that He had sworn to their fathers. And not a man of all their enemies stood against them; the LORD delivered all their enemies into their hand. Not a word failed of any good thing which the LORD had spoken to the house of Israel. All came to pass."*

We see the Israelites as God's people (in a covenant relationship with him), in God's place (living in the Promised Land – Canaan), and under God's rule and enjoying his blessings of grace.

In short, God's people were experiencing some form of rest in God's kingdom. Yet, in the book of Joshua, Joshua cautions the people that they must remember to keep their hearts focused on their King.

Read Joshua 23:6-8; 11-13; 16.

Israel's continued presence before the Lord depended on their obedience (the loyalty of their heart). Otherwise, they would be exiled from the Promised Land - just as Adam and Eve were exiled from the garden. They would no longer experience the blessings that come from dwelling with God.

In Joshua 23:8, the people are told to *"hold fast to the Lord your God, as you have done to this day."* The word "hold fast" is the same word for "cleave" used to describe the union of Adam and Eve in Gen. 2:24. Joshua is likening the picture of our relationship to God with the intimate picture of marriage.[17]

God requires obedience from his covenant people. But the obedience God desires is not external adherence, but an internal identity; the King wants to rule the hearts of his people. For those of us in a covenant relationship with Christ, we are called to keep him first in our lives. As the King's daughters, we are to serve no other god. Obedience is a heart issue; it involves the loyalty of the heart.

We saw this expectation for loyalty of the heart in the giving of the Ten Commandments. The Law was not a sign of outward conformity, but a sign of inner conformity – revealing the state of an individual's heart. When my boys disobey me, they are revealing to me that their hearts are fixed on themselves. Their actions communicate where their true loyalty lies. When my dear friend disregarded God's Word for biblical faithful relationships, she was communicating the depths of her heart, that something and someone other than the King could meet her needs and bring her happiness. Joshua warns the people against this false notion.

THE LINE OF KINGS

God knew the hearts of his people and their shortcomings. He knew when they would finally enter his land and that they would not be satisfied living solely under the rule of God. He knew they would want an earthly king as well – a leader like Moses or Joshua whom they could see, hear, and touch. The people didn't want to be different from the nations surrounding them. They wanted to look like the other nations possessing a monarchy - not the theocracy that God intended, where his subjects would live directly under his Word and live as his vice-regents over the kingdom.

Read Deuteronomy 17:14-20.

And so, before the people ever entered Canaan and displaced its evil inhabitants, God laid out provisions for them to have a king. The king must be chosen by God and be a follower of God.

Definition: King – a male monarch of a major territory who ruled for life, functioning as a military leader and supreme judge over his people.[18]

Significance: The Israelites demand for a human king indicated a waning trust in God alone for their welfare and security and a desire to be like the surrounding nations.[19]

In the book of **Judges**, we see all the events leading up to a king for Israel. The people lived in a devastating cycle of sin from which God continually rescued them. Here's what their pattern of disobedience looked like. Phase 1: they would turn from God and serve false gods. Phase 2: God would then correct them (judge them) by letting them experience defeat by their enemies. Phase 3: after the people demonstrated a change of heart, God rescued them.

Remember, we learned earlier that the final consequence of disobedience was expulsion from the land. But God was long-suffering, waiting on Israel to fulfill their role as a light to the nations. And so when Israel, suffering under the blight of foreign dominance, cried out to the Lord, he mercifully saved them by giving them a temporary military leader (a judge) to help restore peace and rest to the land. But these periods of grace were always provisional. And so the book of Judges chronicles a dark period in Israelite history.

We all have those dark periods in our personal histories. Even as we are the King's daughters, we still struggle with sin and we will continue to do so until he returns once again. But thankfully, God does not leave us to our own strength to keep our heart fixed on him. Just like he did for Israel, God is always faithful to remind us of his promises.

In **1 Samuel**, we see that God finally grants Israel their request and gives them a king. Saul is the first king of the Israelites. However, Saul turns away from God, and the people do not experience the blessings of God's rule.

Second Samuel chronicles the ascension of Israel's second King – David. David is an imperfect man who still fulfills those royal requirements mentioned earlier in Deut. 17. He is chosen by God and he tries to follow God – showing his heart's loyalty.

Under David's rule, the city of Jerusalem is established as the capital of the nation, and it quickly becomes the center of God's kingdom rule. It is the center of worship as the ark of the tabernacle is brought here. And so, the reader is not surprised when David desires to build a temple – a permanent dwelling place – for God in Jerusalem.

Read 2 Samuel 7:1-17.

In this iconic passage, God confirms that the covenant promises given to Abraham are passed to David. Biblical scholar Frank Gaebelein says that verses 9-11 form "a clear echo" of the Abrahamic covenant. Like Abraham, God promises to make the name of David "great," situate Israel in a special "place," and give David "rest."[20]

But alongside those Abrahamic promises of being God's people in God's land and experiencing God's blessing, God gives David additional promises. So, let's look at those promises. They are two-fold.

God will fulfill his promises through David (2 Sam. 7:11). It is through David (his lineage) that God will fulfill his promises and restore creation. God will build a 'house' for David, literally translated 'royal dynasty' (2 Sam. 7:11).

God's promises are eternal (2 Sam. 7:12-14). God promised to build a royal dynasty from David's "Seed" that would last forever and relate to him in a special way (2 Sam. 13-14). The eternal nature of God's promises to David point to a spiritual kingdom. Specifically, the eternality of the prophecy declares a better King is coming. Revisit verse 12: *"When your days are fulfilled and you rest with your fathers, I will set up your seed after you, who will come from your body, and I will establish his kingdom."*

Can you guess what Hebrew word is used in verse 12? The same word for seed (Heb. *'zera*) – that first appeared in God's promise to Adam and Eve in Gen. 3:15.

And while the author of 2 Samuel could have used 'seed' to mean that God would bless multiple Davidic descendants, I believe he is clearly referencing a specific person. Why? Verse 12 says God will establish *his* kingdom. Furthermore, this same person will build a house for God in verse 13.

Many scholars believe the person, the Seed, referenced in this verse to be Solomon. The evidence is indeed compelling. Solomon would later build God a grand house, the temple in Jerusalem. At the end of his life, Solomon is chastened by God because he neglects the Lord's command in Deut. 17 and marries foreign wives (2 Sam. 7:14).

However, we see that the throne of David will be eternal despite Solomon's mistakes. The kingdom/throne of David will continue to persist as it was established by God 'forever.'

So, is 2 Sam. 7 solely fulfilled in Solomon as the Seed of David? Or does it refer to someone else? The New Testament writers clearly understood this passage to refer to Christ. They believed Jesus Christ to be the final fulfillment of the house of David.[21] In Galatians 3:16, Paul specifically refers to the 'seed' as Jesus Christ. In Hebrews 1, the author quotes this exact passage to refer to Jesus Christ. In Luke 1:32-33, the angel Gabriel tells Mary that the son she bears in her womb is the Son of God who holds the throne of David.

So, there is no contradiction between the Old Testament and the New Testament understanding of this passage. We can safely say that the author specifically refers to Solomon in this passage, but that Christ – coming through the seed of David and Solomon and as the Son of the Father– will ultimately establish the house of David forever.

The story continues in **1 Kings** as Solomon takes the throne at the death of his father. During Solomon's reign, Israel experiences a golden age. Just as God said, Solomon builds a glorious temple in Jerusalem for the Lord to dwell in the midst of his people (1 Kings 6; 2 Chron. 3).

In this book, we see that God's covenant continues. Israel is *God's people* (the covenant reaffirmed through David's line), in *God's place* (finally dwelling in the promised land in the city of God in which God himself dwells), and under *God's rule and blessing* (the people experience peace secured by Solomon and have a means to worship in the law and a godly king to lead them).

At last, the people have been given rest. But we will soon see their rest is fleeting. In fact, Israel is about to reach a breaking point as King Solomon's hearts wanders from his King.

DISOBEDIENCE & DIVISION

God's People Disobey

With perhaps his father's dying words ringing in his ears, Solomon marries many foreign wives (1 Kings 2:3). A politically and strategically-motivated decision reaps disastrous consequences, as Solomon succumbs to worshipping the false gods of his wives (2 Kings 11). What was the required punishment if the people began to worship false gods and turn away from their covenant relationship with God? They would be exiled from God's land and his presence and they would experience curses – removal from the blessings of God.

Biblical counselor and author Paul David Tripp puts it this way: when Solomon remains within the boundaries of God's law, "he will prosper. God's way is a way of unique and fulfilling and eternal blessing. There is a beautiful reward, both now and for all of eternity, if we stay within his boundaries."[22]

The King's heart loyalties shifted from God to himself, and like Eve and so many of his ancestors before him, Solomon falls prey to the lie that he was capable of seeking out and determining the "good" of life on his own. As a result, God judges Israel, and the people are divided.

God's People Divided

After 120 years of relative peace and unity, God's people are fractured. Civil war breaks out in Israel and the nation splits in two. Israel becomes the Northern kingdom (comprised of 10 tribes) and the Southern kingdom (comprised of Judah and Benjamin).

Key to the split is the location of Jerusalem in the South. Remember, Jerusalem was designated as the city of God. It housed the temple where the people met God, worshiped him, and made atonement for their sins through sacrifices. For those now living in the North (the majority of the tribes of Israel), they are now separated from God in a sense – both geographically (as the land was the fulfillment of his covenant promise) and spiritually (without temple access they are unable to worship God).

So the king of the North, Jeroboam, provided a "solution." He creates two golden calves in two cities.

Read 1 Kings 12:25-33.

Does this story sound familiar? We already studied how God rescued his people out of Egypt in Ex. 32:4. Aaron, the brother of Moses, said this same thing to the people after giving them a golden calf to worship while Moses was away. Moses would later return with the Ten Commandments (the Law) and set the people right.

Can you see the pattern? This is not just a pattern of idolatry, but ever since the Garden of Eden, man displays a pattern of thought that sets man up to be the authority, deciding how the good in life should be obtained. These parameters always fall outside the boundaries of God's rule – and of course – God's blessing.

From **2 Kings through 2 Chronicles**, we learn that the people finally forced God's hand. At this point in the biblical story, God's people had thoroughly abandoned their role as a light to the nations reflecting what a restful life in God's kingdom looked like.

They no longer considered themselves God's people (having rejected God's covenant relationship) or under God's rule and blessing (having chosen the path of disobedience and curses). And now, just as God declared from the beginning, they would no longer be in God's place – in the Promised Land – enjoying his presence.

Remember, God made these promises to Abraham (Gen. 15:13-16). Moses conveyed these promises to the people (Deut. 28:25, 63-54), and Joshua outlined them again before they entered into the Promised Land (Josh. 23:12-13). Later, God would retell these special promises to David (2 Sam. 7:14). The people had been duly warned.

Being true to his word, the people were exiled from God – scattered among pagan nations that would harshly dominate them. In 722 BC, Assyrians attacked the Northern kingdom (see 2 Kings 17:7), and in 597 BC, Babylonians attacked the Southern kingdom (Judah).

But this is not the end of the story! God's promises are based on his covenant. They are based on God's ability as the strong party to fulfill them, and his promises were "eternal."

Sometimes our own life stories hit an all-time low. They can quickly become dark and painful. Our circumstances can be the way they are because of our own foolish actions like our own self-love. But all too often, our stories hit snags or take dark twists because of someone else's actions against us. A coworker throws us under the bus. A husband leaves. A trusted friend makes public private pains that were shared in confidence. A person from our past that we'd like to forget suddenly resurfaces to reopen old wounds.

But just like Israel, for those of us who are in a covenant relationship with God, our present situations are not the final fulfillment of God's promises to us. Whatever difficulties you are presently dealing with – they are not the end of your story. God can and does redeem us from those situations arising from our own disobedience or foolishness, if we let him. He is our King, and he will never give up or turn away from his covenant promises.

And while our rescue is not always immediate or in the way we expect, God is always faithful. The biblical story is our present proof that the God who is Good will continue to provide for his people in the midst of the exile. Our King is good.

God would continue to speak to his people through a group of men. This group of men understood that God's promises had not yet been completely fulfilled. These men were called prophets. And in the next chapter, we will look at these men and their message.

But first, I want you to see how the History Books end. The Hebrew canon is ordered differently than our English Bibles. If you look at the table of contents in your Bible, you'll see the Old Testament ends with the book of Malachi. Not so with the Hebrew Bible.

The Hebrew canon ends with the History Books at 2 Chronicles. And at the end of 2 Chronicles, a pagan King (Cyrus of Persia) releases the Israelites back to their land and promises to build them a "house." Second Chronicles 36:23 says, *"Thus says Cyrus king of Persia: All the kingdoms of the earth the LORD God of heaven has given me. And He has commanded me to build Him a house at Jerusalem which is in Judah. Who is among you of all His people? May the LORD his God be with him, and let him go up!"*

This passage magnifies the hope of the Jews in the promised Seed – the seed that would come from the "house" of David. God's people expected a royal dynasty, and so the reader is not surprised when the New Testament opens with the book of Matthew which identifies the Seed as Jesus Christ – one who comes from the royal "house" of David.

CONCLUSION

The golden age of Israel is over, but this is not the end of Israel's story. God never intended for this golden age under David and Solomon to be the final fulfillment of his covenant relationship with his people. Because even at its height of glory, the relationship between God and his people at the time of David was still imperfect, still less than intimate, still temporary.

My Story:

God requires obedience from his covenant people.

For those of us already in a covenant relationship with Christ, we are called to keep him first in our hearts. He is to be our first love, meaning we are to serve no other god – especially ourselves. Our decisions, our emotions, our thoughts, our words should all be filtered through the grid of Jesus Christ. When he transforms us, he transforms us completely – every last part, every last thought.

Do you have trouble reconciling obedience with God's grace? Obedience is a heart issue. When Christ changes us, he gives us a heart to help us keep him first. That's not to say we won't ever wander. We aren't perfect. No one is. But as a Daughter of the King, we can count on the resources of faith given to us through our good and kind King who promises to finish the work he's begun and to give us strength while we wait.

For those in a covenant relationship with God, our present situations are not the final fulfillment of God's promises to us.

Whatever difficulties you are presently dealing with – they are not the end of your story. Your story has already been written, and redemption is the climactic event God has planned for those who place their trust in him.

The biblical story is proof that God is still at work in our lives, in your life. God is actively pursuing us to save us from our sin, to save us from our nature, our choices, and our wayward hearts. He is at work to restore us back to him and restore his image in us that was corrupted by sin. Our stories have no cliffhangers; God will continue to work in our lives until we fulfill our created purpose – to be a Daughter of the King.

Like David and Solomon, there will be bumps along the way. Even in grand palaces and plush throne rooms, there are heartaches, losses, and heavy burdens to bear. But the loveliness of our royal status reflects on the King who gives us rest rather than the privileged status he extends.

This is what I've learned from watching my kids battle their desires and my sweet friend battle false beliefs about her King. The King draws his children out of the cycles of sin and gives them a special role in his kingdom for a grand purpose. Our role as Daughters of the King – when undertaken with a whole and loyal heart - serves to point others to his kingdom.

Chapter 5: The King's Subjects Demand a King

1. How would you describe disobedience? What does your own life choices reveal about the loyalty of your heart? How does Christ help you obey God's commands?

2. According to Deut. 17:14-20, what are some of the qualities of a King? What did Israel's desire for a King reveal about the loyalty of their hearts?

3. In 2 Sam. 7, God makes a covenant with David. Compare the covenant God made with Abraham to the covenant he made with David.

4. What happened to Israel as a result of the divided loyalties of Solomon's heart?

At the end of the History Books, Israel hits an all-time low. Describe a time when your life story hit an all-time low. How did God redeem your situation for his glory? Are you at an all-time low even as you read this? What promise from this chapter can you cling to help you better orient your heart to the King?

CHAPTER 6: THE KING'S PROPHETS
THE WRITINGS AND THE PROPHETS

Without a doubt, there is one question that makes my skin scrawl faster than any other: *"I've got good news and bad news. Which one do you want first?"*

I hate the question because it puts me a no-win situation. If I choose to hear the good news first, then I get to enjoy the good news, but I'm left holding the bad news. On the other hand, if I choose to hear the bad news first I end up on a good note, but there's no delaying my confrontation with the bad news. And bad news casts a long, dark shadow.

In the previous chapter, we ended our lesson on a rather depressing point in Israel's history. A shadow of bad news had been cast over God's people. We learned from the History Books (Joshua – Esther) that Israel rejected the gracious rule of God's kingdom in lieu of self-rule and their disobedience resulted in separation from God, expulsion from the land, and slavery to cruel nations. It doesn't really seem that it could get any darker than that.

And bearing this dark news, were certain men commissioned by God with a good news/bad news message. These men were called **prophets**, and they understood that the golden age of Israel under David and Solomon was not the end of God's story for his people. God intended a complete, perfect, and eternal restoration of his kingdom through a coming King. The prophets knew the promises that were fulfilled during the golden age were only partially fulfilled. An even greater Kingdom, yet to be seen, was in their future.

This was the good news, but the bad news was the people still had to account for their sin. They could not continue with wayward hearts that rejected the King while still enjoying the blessings of his kingdom.

> **Definition**: **Prophet** – A human messenger called to speak God's Word to God's people and call them back to their covenant relationship.[23]
>
> **Significance**: Prophets enforced Israel's covenant with God urging the people to respond to the gift of salvation in obedience by repenting of their sin.

There were many prophets throughout the Old Testament. In this chapter, we'll be looking at some of these chosen men and their messages, primarily recorded in the Writings (Job - Song of Solomon) and the Prophets (Isaiah – Malachi).

THE MEN

The prophets prophesied before, during, and after the exile. God was long-suffering (slow to anger) with Israel, patiently waiting for the nation to repent of their idolatry and submit themselves to his rule again. He desperately wanted them to resume their rightful role as his vice-regents in his kingdom – his priests to the nations. And so God sent many different men in many different time periods to try to enforce his covenant.

I think this chart is helpful for organizing these men:[24]

kingdom	Before Exile – 8 B.C.	During Exile – 7 B.C.	After Exile – 6 B.C.
North (Israel)	Amos Hosea		
South (Judah)	Isaiah	Jeremiah	Haggai

	Micah	Ezekiel	Zechariah
	Joel	Daniel	Malachi
	Nahum	Obadiah	
		Zephaniah	

Like he does with his daughters today, God gives his people numerous chances to repent. In the case of Israel, he gave them centuries to respond to his word. Today, God's dealings with us are similar. And although our covenant relationship to God is founded on his Son, we still see that God desperately desires for us to come to him and enjoy the blessings of dwelling with him.

We often think of the message of the Old Testament prophets as gloom and doom. And it is largely, as we'll soon see, but that message of doom and gloom is purposed to protect us – to urge us to remain faithful to our faithful God, to urge us to remain loyal to his rule over our hearts so that we might fulfill the special calling he's placed on our lives.

THE MESSAGE

So, let's look at the message of these men. Like two sides of a coin, the prophets conveyed two messages. In fact, you could say that these two messages were essentially the same message.

Judgment

Because sin is pervasive – present in all men and impacting all creation – the whole earth must be called into account and judged. It is not just Israel who disobeyed God, but all men have chosen wickedness and, therefore, are deserving of death. *Romans 5:12 says, "Therefore, just as through one man sin entered the world, and death through sin, and thus death spread to all men, because all sinned…"*

But God's judgment on the Israelites is particularly important because they were called to a special task (to be a light to the nations) and given special privileges of living with a holy God. God gave the Israelites hundreds of years to fulfill their task and enjoy him. Additionally, he gave them clear warnings of the consequences their disobedience would incur (his judgment). We read about that in the previous chapter (Josh. 23). Today, we might think these judgments don't matter to us. But they do!

The prophets' message <u>warns us</u> of the importance of obedience and faithfulness to our covenant relationship with God. Later in this study, we'll see exactly what our covenant relationship with God looks like and what it entails. But at this point, I just want to stress that we are still required to be faithful to God. He is after our hearts. Remember from Josh. 23, the author urges the people to "cleave" to the Lord's Words, calling to mind the marriage union of Adam and Eve in Gen. 2:24.

The prophets' message <u>foreshadows</u> a more terrible judgment to come. God gave the Israelites plenty of forewarning of the curses they would reap if they rejected his kingdom rule. And so today, God gives the world plenty of forewarning on that final, impending judgment. In chapter 10, we'll look more at this final judgment.

But the prophets' message doesn't just foreshadow gloom; they foreshadow hope! If all men outside the kingdom (outside a covenant relationship with God) are to be judged for sin, then we know that all those found inside the kingdom (inside a covenant relationship with God) are to be saved by his promise in Genesis 3:15, in which all evil is destroyed forever.

Hope

For those found inside God's covenant relationship, judgment is not the end!

So while the Israelites forfeited blessings and received judgment due to their disobedience, it doesn't mean their covenant relationship is over. The blessings of the covenant relationship may disappear, but God's covenant does not! And so, the prophets speak of a great hope – a final restoration for God's people.

The promises are three-fold and align with both the Abrahamic and Davidic covenants: God's people, in God's place, under God's rule and blessing. These promises are strewn across the pages of the Prophets and Writings. I'll highlight just enough to give you the big picture.

God's People

The first promise of God as delivered by the prophets focuses on the identity of God's people. It includes four components: (1) God will preserve a remnant of faithful Israelites, (2) bring them out of slavery from exile in a new exodus, (3) provide salvation for them by the hand of a

Suffering Servant whose atoning work is so comprehensive that it will (4) extend to all nations.

A Remnant Preserved

Judgment for sin is certain. Isaiah, who prophesied before the exile, promised the people as much. Listen to Isaiah 10, and try to discern the message of hope.

"And it shall come to pass in that day
That the remnant of Israel,
And such as have escaped of the house of Jacob,
Will never again depend on him who defeated them,
But will depend on the Lord, the Holy One of Israel, in truth.
The remnant will return, the remnant of Jacob,
To the Mighty God." (Is. 10:20-21)

Through the prophet Isaiah, God promises that a small group of Israelites would be saved from the exile. This small group, called a 'remnant,' would remain faithful to God during the impending exile, and they would be sustained through their suffering. As a result, they would lay hold of God's ultimate blessings.

This remnant is an important concept because our studies in Gen. 3:15 and 2 Sam. 7 have shown us that God's people were promised a King, a Seed of David, that would rule them forever. The promised King was expected to come from this remnant. In Is. 10:21, the prophet says the "remnant of Jacob" will return to "the Mighty God." The term "Jacob" begs the reader to remember the origin of the promised Messiah in Gen. 49, and the term "Mighty God" reminds us of Isaiah's earlier description of the King in Is. 9:6.[25]

The remnant would be preserved by a specific person – a royal King with a divine nature.

A New Exodus

Through the prophet Jeremiah, God promises to save the people from slavery and restore them to the land of their forefathers.

"Therefore behold, the days are coming," says the Lord, "that it shall no more be said, 'The Lord lives who brought up the children of Israel from the land of Egypt,' but, 'The Lord lives who brought up the children of Israel from the land of the north and from all the lands where He had driven them.' For I will bring them back into their land which I gave to their fathers." (Jer. 16:14-15).

There is much packed into these verses. Our minds are trained to only read of God's physical salvation from bondage, but remember that returning to the land meant a place to dwell with God. So, while God's people most certainly felt God had abandoned them in exile, in Jeremiah's words they would have heard God telling them he will return to them himself. The people would have understood Jeremiah's message of hope – a promise of redemption from a life of slavery under foreign rule and restoration to the loving rule of a coming King.

A Suffering Servant

Also through the prophet Isaiah, God promised that Israel will be rescued, not by a majestic rule like the judges or King David or Solomon, but by a Servant whose rule is characterized by suffering.

"Behold! My Servant whom I uphold,
My Elect One in whom My soul delights!
I have put My Spirit upon Him;
He will bring forth justice to the Gentiles.
He will not cry out, nor raise His voice,
Nor cause His voice to be heard in the street." (Is. 42:1-2)

Isaiah reveals that God's Servant would be anointed by the very Spirit of God (Is. 44:1-2). He would be a humble figure who is exalted over the nations through his suffering (Is. 52:13-15). And most importantly, he would bear the sins of his people by acting as a substitute sacrifice (Is. 53:5-6). He is pierced, crushed, and bears God's wrath in our place (Is. 5-6).[26]

"But He was wounded for our transgressions,
He was bruised for our iniquities;
The chastisement for our peace was upon Him,
And by His stripes we are healed.
All we like sheep have gone astray;
We have turned, every one, to his own way;
And the Lord has laid on Him the iniquity of us all." (Is. 53:5-6)

The rescue of God's people occurs by means of the death of the coming King. And so you see an ironic twist as the Suffering Servant bears the exile of the people in their place – as he is exiled from the Lord.

While we don't want to jump ahead in our story, the reader is left wondering, *"Who is this Suffering Servant?"* While some passages clearly link the faithful remnant of Israel with the Servant, many commentators believe that these passages in Isaiah all point to a specific individual - the promised

Messiah.[27] Indeed, the New Testament authors indicate this truth (Matt. 8:17; 12:17-21; John 12:38; Acts 8:30-35).

The God of all Nations

The reach of the effects of the Suffering Servant are so pervasive that they extend beyond Israel and to all nations.

"Indeed He says,
'It is too small a thing that You should be My Servant
To raise up the tribes of Jacob,
And to restore the preserved ones of Israel;
I will also give You as a light to the Gentiles,
That You should be My salvation to the ends of the earth.' " (Is. 49:6)

"Arise, shine;
For your light has come!
And the glory of the Lord is risen upon you.
For behold, the darkness shall cover the earth,
And deep darkness the people;
But the Lord will arise over you,
And His glory will be seen upon you.
The Gentiles shall come to your light,
And kings to the brightness of your rising." (Is. 60:1-3)

Just as Israel was to be a light to the nations – a kingdom of priests – the Suffering Servant fulfills this role perfectly. As a result all men and women may enter into the promises given to Abraham and David (Is. 60:1-3).

God's Place

The second promise of God given through the prophets centers on the unique place in which God's people were to dwell with him – a new temple and a new creation.

A New Temple

Through the prophet Ezekiel, God revealed that the temple in Jerusalem would be destroyed. The glory of God would depart from it. But Ezekiel (who prophesied during the years of the exile), speaks of a new temple even more magnificent than the first!

"Then he brought me back to the door of the temple; and there was water, flowing from under the threshold of the temple toward the east, for the front of the temple faced east; the water was flowing from under the right side of the temple, south of the altar…And it shall

be that every living thing that moves, wherever the rivers go, will live. There will be a very great multitude of fish, because these waters go there; for they will be healed, and everything will live wherever the river goes." (Ezek. 47:1, 9)

This new temple has a river flowing out of it giving life to the world. Please file that thought away for later! This imagery will return later in the biblical story. For now, simply remember this promise and that it means God's people would have a life-giving place to dwell with him.

A New Creation

"For behold, I create new heavens and a new earth;
And the former shall not be remembered or come to mind.
But be glad and rejoice forever in what I create;
For behold, I create Jerusalem as a rejoicing,
And her people a joy." (Is. 65:17-18)

At the end of the book of Isaiah, the prophet gives God's people a view of the ultimate end of God's creation and God's people – all will be restored to him by being recreated. And this second creation will be eternal (Is. 65:18). Isaiah says this new creation will be so incredible that the old way of life will no longer be remembered – a sure hope to the remaining Israelites suffering in exile at the time this was written.

But the entire chapter of Is. 65 serves as context for verses 17-18. Before God can restore the world and restore his kingdom, he must first conquer evil. Therefore, restoration will be preceded by warnings of judgment and a call for salvation. No one can say they were not warned in time to repent.

God's Rule and Blessing

While the first promise focused on God's people and the second promise centered on God's place, God's third promise delivered by the prophets emphasizes the blessings of living under God's rule. The third promise includes the idea of a new covenant and a new King.

A New Covenant

Better than any other prophet, Jeremiah knew Israel's covenant with God was, at the time, far from perfect. That's because the results from the first covenant never lasted. God's people consistently sinned, were exiled from the presence of a holy God, and forfeited the covenant blessings that were promised to them upon obedience. They needed help to fulfill their obligations to their covenant relationship with God. It is Jeremiah who delivers the good news: God's answer is to help his people in their obedience by fulfilling the old covenant for them.

"Behold, the days are coming, says the Lord, when I will make <u>a new covenant</u> with the house of Israel and with the house of Judah— not according to the covenant that I made with their fathers in the day that I took them by the hand to lead them out of the land of Egypt, My covenant which they broke, though I was a husband to them, says the Lord. But this is the covenant that I will make with the house of Israel after those days, says the Lord: I will put My law in their minds, and write it on their hearts; and I will be their God, and they shall be My people." (Jer. 31:31-33)

God promises his people a new covenant. In the same way that he isn't abolishing the Law, he is not abolishing the old covenant. Rather, God is going to offer his people a better means for fulfillment. He is going to write his Law on their hearts (Ezek. 31:33, 36:26-27); he is going to change them from within.[28]

Both Ezekiel and Joel make it clear that this is a promise of the presence of God's Holy Spirit in the lives of all people (Joel 2:28-32).

So while the new covenant still contains the Law of God, now it will be internalized (Rom. 3:31). Later in the biblical story we'll see how the internalization of the Law takes place – through Christ who fulfills the Law on our behalf.

A New King

The prophets linked the promise of this new covenant with the promise of a coming King. There is perhaps no other passage of Scripture more poetic than Is. 9:6-7. The fact that it is typically only sung and read during the Christmas season is great tragedy because the prophet's greater message encompasses more than the birth of a small child but the rise of a great and divine King.

"For unto us a Child is born,
Unto us a Son is given;
And the government will be upon His shoulder.
And His name will be called
Wonderful, Counselor, Mighty God,
Everlasting Father, Prince of Peace.
Of the increase of His government and peace
There will be no end,
Upon the throne of David and over His kingdom,
To order it and establish it with judgment and justice
From that time forward, even forever.

The zeal of the Lord of hosts will perform this." (Is. 9:6-7)

This new King is set apart from the royal heirs of the earth. Because unlike any of Israel's sons, the King is universally authoritative, he is peace, he is God, and he is eternal.

We've already noted that the royal imagery of a promised Seed dots the landscape of the biblical story beginning as early as Gen. 17 with God's promise that a King will come from Abraham and Sarah's Seed and running through to Gen. 49 with Jacob's blessing on the tribe of Judah. We've seen how God assembled a kingdom of priests who were to be ruled by a divine King (Ex. 19). And, we traced the royal motif to David to whom God transferred and expanded the Abrahamic covenant (2 Sam. 7:12-16). So, no one is surprised to see the same promises of a coming King surface in the prophets like Isaiah and even Daniel.[29]

These promises of a new covenant, a new heart, a new King are also present in the Writings, many of which were penned by David who held these promises close to his heart. Psalm 2 is one such song of hope.

"Yet I have set My King
On My holy hill of Zion.
'I will declare the decree:
The Lord has said to Me,
'You are My Son,
Today I have begotten You.
Ask of Me, and I will give You
The nations for Your inheritance,
And the ends of the earth for Your possession.
You shall break them with a rod of iron;
You shall dash them to pieces like a potter's vessel.'
Now therefore, be wise, O kings;
Be instructed, you judges of the earth.
Serve the Lord with fear,
And rejoice with trembling.
Kiss the Son, lest He be angry,
And you perish in the way,
When His wrath is kindled but a little.
Blessed are all those who put their trust in Him." (Ps. 2:6-12).

Ps. 2 embodies the good news/bad news scenario seen in the prophets – the news of judgment and hope. The loveliness of the song is found in the way it ends – on a note of intimacy. The idea of "kissing" the son is a call to an intimate relationship with the Son, the coming King. We see terms of endearment and devotion used here that seem discordant with the grotesque pictures of judgment. But remember, the message found in both is like a two-sided coin.

Our blessings are intimately tied to the coming King. Many of the blessings that we've outlined in the prophets - a new covenant, a new temple, a new creation – are all contingent upon the coming King and the status of our relationship to him. And so, even today, we are called to place our hope in this very same King.

CONCLUSION

There is great hope in the prophets. The prophets knew their words of hope hinged on the people's faithfulness, and so we cannot separate their sentiment from their words of warning.

In 538 BC, the Israelites would need these words more than ever. Cyrus of Persia would defeat the Babylonians and release the Jews. A remnant of God's people returns to Jerusalem and the temple and their city is rebuilt. The process is long and difficult, and the end result is not nearly as glorious as they remembered.

My Story:

God desires I come to him in repentance so I might enjoy the blessings of his covenant.

God gives us the time and opportunity to repent of our sin and place our trust in him. In the same way that God gave the Israelites many chances to place their trust in him alone, so he is longsuffering with us. In the coming chapters, we will discuss how we enter into a relationship with God. We hinted at it in this chapter. God provides a new covenant – a new way – in which to relate to him as his people. It is available to all people and is his work exclusively.

My blessings are intimately tied to the coming King.

Just like Israel, we are asked to trust in God to fulfill all the promises made to those who are in a covenant with him. God's promises hinge on the coming King.

As the Old Testament closes, the reader is left to fix her eyes on the future. Mal. 3:1 says, *"See, I will send my messenger, who will prepare the way before me.*

Then suddenly the Lord you are seeking will come to his temple; the messenger of the covenant, whom you desire, will come,' says the LORD Almighty."

And so the people are left to wait for the messenger to herald the good news of the arrival of the coming King – the King who would inaugurate the new covenant, the new temple, the new kingdom. And so shall we…wait until the next chapter to discover the identity of the coming King and his messenger!

Chapter 6: The King's Prophets

1. Describe the role of God's prophets in the Old Testament and their significance for God's people.

2. Like two sides to a coin, the prophets' message was two-fold. Briefly describe their message of judgment.

3. We discussed eight hope-filled promises communicated by the prophets. Which promise speaks to your heart today, and why?

4. The Prophets of the Old Testament told the people that their blessings were tied intimately to the coming King. One day, a King would come who would be their perfect King, and this King would bless them in a more permanent and perfect way. (A) Read Eph. 1:3 and describe the scope of the blessings this King gives to his daughters today. (B) Then make a list of all the blessings listed in Eph. 1:1-14 that you currently enjoy because of your relationship with King Jesus.

Reflect on the blessings you've received as a Daughter of the King (as listed from Eph. 1:1-14). What role did you play in obtaining any of these blessings? Describe a time when you tried to obtain a blessing (whether spiritual or physical) from God on your own terms, and the result.

CHAPTER 7: THE KING COMES
THE GOSPELS

Growing up, I was enthralled with the story Cinderella. I must have watched the animated classic a million times. But my favorite part, besides the cute little dancing mice, was when Cinderella's fairy godmother magically transformed the lowly house servant into a beautiful maiden solely by changing her dress. The animated scene is full of glitter and wonder as the fairy godmother goes to work exchanging Cinderella's tattered rags for a sparkling ball gown.

Our stories as Daughters of the King are similar. Before Christ, we wear our sins publicly, and they are ugly. And if we were to look into a mirror, we would discover the light of the Law reveals them to be even dirtier than we imagine. But when the King *transforms* our hearts through his Spirit, we are given the most *beautiful garments of salvation* to wear.[30]

This chapter is a pivotal part of the biblical story. The previous six chapters have taken us on a whirlwind ride through the Old Testament, and now we begin our tour of the New Testament's perspective of the promises of God. So far in our story, we've seen God establish his pattern for his kingdom: a restful rule enjoyed by his sub-regents, mankind. We've seen how sin marred that pattern and how all of life needs to be restored back to God's original design.

And in God's grace, the restoration process began immediately after Adam and Eve sinned. God promised the first couple that one day he would totally destroy evil (Gen. 3:15). To Adam and Eve's descendants (their 'seed'), God fleshed out his promise in three ways:

Mankind would be *God's people* (enjoying a covenant relationship with the King).

Mankind would be in *God's place* (dwelling in a specific land with the King).

Mankind would be under *God's rule and blessings* (given freely when the people remained under the King's rule).

But because sin's effects are so pervasive, mankind struggled to remain faithful to God's standards and was continually exiled from their precious land and the King's presence. But our God is a good God, and despite the sin of his people, he would or did not forsake them. He brought back a remnant of the people to the land and intended to give them a special King – but not just any king – a Messiah, the Seed of salvation.

It is this King who exchanges our tattered, filthy rags for garments of righteousness. It is this King who transforms us from a lowly sinner to a Daughter of the King.

EXPECTING A KING - INTERTESTAMENTAL PERIOD

Before we begin looking at the Gospels, it is important to see where the Jewish hearts were at that time.

Between the last book in the Old Testament (Malachi) and the first book in the New Testament (Matthew), there is a long lapse of time – 400 years to be precise. And during this time there were no prophets.

The last recorded word from God came in the 5th century B.C. from Malachi. Mal. 3:1 says, " *'Behold, I send My messenger, And he will prepare the way before Me. And the Lord, whom you seek, Will suddenly come to His temple, Even the Messenger of the covenant, In whom you delight. Behold, He is coming,' Says the Lord of hosts.* "

Can you imagine hearing direct words from God through his prophets on a regular basis, and then nothing for 400 years? God's people must have felt abandoned. They must have felt duped, angry, and a little disillusioned. They must have been tempted to doubt the good King and his good promises.

But God is always at work in our lives even when he seems to be silent. As his daughters, we can trust in God's promises even when we can't see how they will ever come to pass in our lives. That's because his covenant with us, as his daughters, is eternal. It is based on God's ability as the stronger party to uphold his agreement, not on our ability. Even in silence, we know God is at work and God is good.

Despite God's silence, the Jews continued to look for this messenger prophesied in Mal. 3:1, the messenger who would herald the coming of the Messiah. And the timing of the messenger's arrival couldn't have been better. A remnant had returned to the land, a new temple had been built – all that God's people needed was the glory of the Lord to return to his temple. Now they just needed God to raise up their promised King.

During this period, Israel would have many rulers, but none who would usher in the new covenant. In fact, this time was a desolate time for Israel. They were brutally dominated by foreign governments, including Persia, the Greeks under Alexander the Great, Egypt under the leadership of the Ptolemies and the dreadful Antiochus IV, and lastly the Roman Empire.

The Jews knew they were destined to be led by a King of their own, a son of David. But instead, for 400 more years, they were oppressed by foreign governments. So, by the time the book of Matthew opens in the first century, Jewish hope for the arrival of the Messiah is at a feverish pitch.

But if there's one thing the biblical story proves it's that God's timing is perfect. God fulfills his purpose in his timing, and we shall see that God's timing is always on time.

THE ARRIVAL OF THE KING

Let's begin where the New Testament begins – in the book of Matthew.

Read Matthew 1:1-17.

Matthew opens with a long list of family names. Much of this information may seem boring to you. But in some of my undergraduate journalism classes, we were taught to make the first paragraph of an article, called the lead paragraph, the most interesting part of the story. The lead is intended to draw the reader into the story, and any writer or speaker will concur. The first few sentences are crucial to securing your readers attention, right? So, why does Matthew start with genealogy?

In opening his book with a long genealogy, Matthew has a special purpose. He is connecting the Old Testament promises of a coming King to the person of Jesus Christ. Matthew is carefully tracing the lineage of Jesus Christ from Abraham to David! He is legitimizing Jesus Christ as the royal heir to the Davidic throne.[31]

The biblical story finally reveals the identity of the Seed – the promised

King! But this genealogy also serves another purpose besides establishing lineage. It is directly positioning Christ as the fulfillment of all the promises given to Abraham.[32]

The wise woman who edited this book told me she likes to read the first line of a novel and then compare it to the very last line in the book. That's a brilliant tactic because you can sense the author's purpose in writing. The beginning of Matthew links Jesus Christ to all nations (1:1), and the last line of Matthew continues this same thought as Jesus commissions his followers to make disciples of all nations. Matthew is making a point: the promised King is not just a ruler for the Israelites, he is the King of all people.

The four **Gospels** (Matthew, Mark, Luke, and John) offer four different eye witness accounts of the life and death of Jesus Christ the King. The word gospel literally means "good news." In fact, it is the very best news we will ever hear; the gospel is the transformative motor driving the biblical story forward.

In this chapter, we are going to weave in and out of the four Gospels to see how Jesus Christ fulfills all those promises presented in the biblical story. I hope this study whets your appetite to further dig into the person and work of Christ. So, be sure to check out the footnotes for additional information and resources. (I'm a book nerd, remember?)

God's People

The Gospels tell us *Christ is the substitute for God's people on earth*. Only Jesus lived a sinless, perfect, obedient life – unlike God's people. The Gospel writers call Christ the beginning of a new humanity. Luke calls Jesus the new Adam, and Matthew subtly likens Jesus to the new Israel – succeeding where both failed (Luke 3:23-28; Matt. 4:1-11; see also 2:15).[33]

God's Place

The Gospels tell us *Christ is the substitute for God's Place as the temple on earth*. Remember the significance of the promise of the land? God's promise to give his people land involved not only a physical place to dwell in rest, but also a place to dwell in the very presence of God. Before sin, Adam and Eve existed in God's presence in a perfect place – the Garden of Eden. Sin caused them to be expelled from both the presence of God and the garden. God's promises to his people involved restoring to them a special place to dwell with him – a special land. Before the people entered into the Promised Land of Canaan, God graciously gave them the tabernacle and later the temple in which to reside in his presence.

But Jesus, as both fully man and fully God, replaces the need for both the temple or the tabernacle. Because Christ came to dwell with men directly, man no longer needs these places in which to worship God. This is glorious news for the King's daughters. The King we serve lives not in a distant land; his kingdom is here and he lives among us.

Read John 1:14.

In John 1:14, we are told that Christ dwells among his people. The word for "dwelt among us" is literally translated 'tabernacled' or "pitch a tent, to dwell temporarily."[34] And so Christ becomes the living, breathing tabernacle on earth.

Read John 2:18-21.

In John 2:18-21, Christ refers to himself as the temple. Interestingly, at the close of the Hebrew Scriptures, the pagan king Cyrus of Persia desires to build a house for the Lord. And then the New Testament opens with much talk in the Gospels about the 'house' of the Lord. Christ identifies himself with the temple (cf. Luke 2:41-52).[35]

Read John 7:37-38.

In John 7:37-38, Christ is the temple through which life comes.[36] Notice the reference to "rivers of living water." Do you remember hearing that before? This image appears earlier in Ezek. 47. Ezekiel the prophet prophesied about a new temple out of which would flow life-giving water.

Undoubtedly, the apostle John knew the Old Testament Scriptures, and he is clearly connecting the prophetic words concerning the new temple with Jesus Christ. Christ physically fulfilled the promise of land to God's people. As such, there is no way to dwell in the presence of God without knowing the King and being under his rule.

Daughters of the King are afforded great blessings – dwelling in a holy and royal place and direct access to the King. We don't have to wait in line or take a ticket in order to get a hearing with the King. We don't have to scrounge to work for special blessings he brings our way. Being a Daughter of the King is more than a lifestyle that brings blessings of royalty; being related to the King *IS* life – eternal life. In Christ we find our position and our privilege – but we also find our life in his presence.

God's Rule

And lastly, the Gospels tell us *Christ is the substitute vice-regent over creation;*

Christ is the King. As divine image-bearers, mankind was intended be God's vice-regent over creation (see chapter 1). But mankind failed to fulfill this important role in God's kingdom. And so, Christ, as the King over creation, fulfills this role on behalf of man.

How so? Christ perfectly submitted to God's rule. He lived and walked on this earth without ever sinning, and, in doing so, secured the blessing of the covenant on our behalf. In short, Christ demonstrates to us what the restored image of God looks like in man – one who lives as God's people, in God's place, under God's rule.

This is why Christ says in Matthew 5:17, *"Do not think that I came to destroy the Law or the Prophets. I did not come to destroy but to fulfill."* The Law was the vehicle through which the Israelites received and experienced God's blessing. Christ fulfilled those requirements perfectly, and now man is no longer bound to the letter of the Law to receive God's blessings. While the Law is not abolished, Christ releases us from the slavery to the Law in order to receive blessings. The new covenant means our blessings are inherited solely through our relationship to Christ.

	God's People	God's Place	God's Rule/Blessing
Old Testament	Israel	The Temple in the Promised Land	The Law
New Testament	Jesus Christ is the new Adam	Jesus Christ is the new Temple	Jesus Christ is the new King over the kingdom

As the King's daughters, we sometimes forget that our blessings come through Christ alone and not by how well we uphold our covenant relationship. This was the missing piece to Israel's relationship to her King. She experienced blessings when she kept her heart's affections centered on the King and forfeited the blessings that came with her privileged position when she strayed. Sin kept Israel living in the tension searching for God's blessing but unable to procure it on her own strength.

Sadly, sometimes I still live in this old covenant mentality. I sometimes believe that the works of my hands will bring me special blessings or special treatment from my King. I battled this legalistic line of thought when my husband and I were trying to have children. I read passages like Ps. 127:3 and knew that children were indeed a blessing from God, a "reward," even. *So, why did God grant the reward of children to so many unwed teenagers and not me?* The thought came out more like a ripe accusation than a true question. I felt like I had played by "all the rules," and coming away from parenthood empty-handed made it seem like God wasn't.

For most of my doctor's appointments, I sat in waiting rooms filled with teen moms in their third trimester. They talked about their dating woes, hot boyfriends, ditching class, and the latest text to circulate the school. When I went back for my second miscarriage, the disparity of these blessings grew so large in my mind that I almost changed doctors.

But God spoke to my heart through a very wise Sunday School teacher. He showed me that while children are indeed a special blessing, they are not the *only* reward God gives his daughters. He pointed to the story of Abraham, who, in his great age, was promised a son. To Abraham, God clearly told him, "I am your…exceedingly great reward" (Gen. 15:1). It was all I needed to hear to convict my heart that I do not need to wrestle blessings away from God. God has already given me the greatest, most previous reward I could desire: himself.

I realized I had fallen prey to the deception that I deserved to be rewarded with a blessing of my own choosing. Worse still, I was guilty of grossly misapplying Christ's work on my behalf. The King desires to bless all his daughters, and indeed he has. Because of God's extravagant love for us realized in the person and work of Jesus Christ, he has already given his daughters every blessing we will ever need. In Eph. 3:1, Paul says, *"Praise be to the God and Father of our Lord Jesus Christ, who has blessed us…"* The Greek emphasizes that these unmerited blessings are already ours to enjoy.

The blessings of living under the King's rule and in his kingdom are not opportunities to be seized, a prosperous destiny to be claimed, or a reward doled out for good behavior. The good gifts we receive in life come from and because of Christ – and this is the really important part – they are already ours to savor and enjoy.

The life of Christ, then, is the literal fulfillment of all the Abrahamic promises. In his life, we see the fulfillment of God's people, living in God's place, under God's rule and blessing. This is why Paul says that all the promises of God find their fulfillment in Christ (2 Cor. 1:20).

This is the new covenant that the prophets hoped for – a way to dwell with God and experience his blessings permanently. So it is not surprising when we see the New Testament open with the messenger, John the Baptist, connecting the arrival of the King with the coming of the kingdom of God.

Matthew 3:1-2 says, *"In those days John the Baptist came preaching in the wilderness of Judea, and saying, 'Repent, for the kingdom of heaven is at hand!'"* This is a message Christ himself preached in Matthew 4:17: *"From that time Jesus began to preach and to say, 'Repent, for the kingdom of heaven is at hand.'"*

Christ is the key to this new covenant, this new kingdom. *But how does that happen exactly?*

THE DEATH OF THE KING

How does this new covenant work? How do we go from being under the Law to being freed from it?

Just as God never changes, so God's plan for salvation has never changed. Salvation has always come through faith and the pattern exemplified in substitutionary atonement. Remember the sacrificial system we discussed in chapter 4? Every Passover lamb and every sacrifice pointed to Christ. Remember the blood required to atone for sins? Justice required an innocent blood sacrifice. And in Christ's death, this requirement is met. This is why John 1:29 states, *"The next day John saw Jesus coming toward him, and said, 'Behold! The Lamb of God who takes away the sin of the world!'"*

Read Hebrews 9:11-27.

Christ is the eternal sacrifice (cf. Heb. 10).[37] It was not enough for Christ to come to earth and "tabernacle" among us. His coming does not completely solve the problem of sin, but his death does because he is the perfect sacrifice. God's righteous wrath against us due to our sin is satisfied in Christ (his blameless life and his innocent death on our behalf.) In Christ's death, the requirement of the Law is met (Rom. 8:1-4) in that Christ bore the penalty for us (2 Cor. 5:21).

Our transformation comes at a painful price. In restoring the image of God within us, there is no light and cheery wave of wand. There is no bibbidi-bobbidi-boo. As foretold by Isaiah, the Messiah suffers excruciatingly so that you and I might enter into a new covenant. The grossness of our sin requires a gross and painful consequence.

But it is through Christ's death that we are able to enter into God's kingdom, to live as God's people in God's place under God's rule and experience his blessings. The death of Christ fulfills the old covenant so that you and I might live in light of the new. But you and I would never have been able to enter into the new covenant without help.

Righteousness and blessing come only through Christ. As the substitute sacrifice for our sins, Christ's righteousness is imputed, or credited, to us. Much like Cinderella, in exchange for the filthy rags we wear, we are given Christ's clean garments. So, when God looks at us, he sees only the brilliant, shining garments of salvation given to us by the King himself.

Yet, we often live our lives according to the old covenant – living lives ruled by legalism and outward behavior, desiring to be a royal yet putting on our own tattered rags. We could never expect to meet God's holy standards without help – without Christ. In Is. 64:6, we learn that *"...we are all like an unclean thing, And all our righteousnesses are like filthy rags..."* In the original Hebrew, the filthy rags to which Isaiah refers are menstrual cloths.[38]

So, why would we want to wear such dirty rags of our making when we could be like Cinderella at the ball – transformed into spectacular linen given to us by our King?

CONCLUSION

My Story:

Through Christ, God will perform his will in my life at the perfect time.

There is nothing that is happening in your life right now that is a surprise to God. Your life circumstances haven't caught him off guard or forced his hand into Plan B. Similarly, God is always on time; he is always at work in our lives even when he is silent.

I spent four very long years praying alongside my dear friend, Amanda, who, above all things, deeply desired to be a mother. Because of my own struggle in this area, we shared many tear-filled conversations on my couch, hands clutching mugs of steaming coffee and hearts refusing to let go of the gift of Christ in our lives. Our conversations formed a familiar melody that would resonate in the lives of women around the globe. Like many women struggling with infertility, my friend battled the lie that she was, in some way, deficient or broken because she was unable to conceive. She battled her Heavenly Father daily on this account, challenging the way he made her and wondering what he had made her for, if not to have children.

Despite our circumstances, Scripture is clear that as his daughters, God made us perfectly. Regardless of health, appearance, or gifts, we are created in the King's very image. And although sin has marred that image within us, our value lies not in what we do, what we look like, or how many children we bear, but in our relationship to our King. He is the one who makes our life valuable. And even when we're suffering from a loss we've never known, we can trust that our exceptional worth as a Daughter of the King remains unchanging. Just like all his daughters, we are all valued, appreciated, treasured, loved, prized, and esteemed by the King. We can also trust that God directs our personal histories, present realities, and even the unknown future toward a good end.

Because our King always has his daughters best interests at heart, we can trust in his perfect timing, too. This doesn't mean that we will be comfortable while we wait for him to reveal his will, Word, or ways to us. But whether we are waiting for rescue or answers, we have the ultimate comfort: we have the eternal King, who is our ultimate and deepest reward.

Christ shows me what the restored image of God in me should look like.

Christ is our example of life in the new kingdom. He perfectly fulfilled all the requirements of the Law on our behalf, perfectly serving as the King (vice-regent) over creation. What we could not and cannot do, he does for us. And in doing so, he frees us from the Law and from the cycles of sins that ensnare us. He shows us what our role on earth is supposed to look like – what God intended for service, love, creative stewardship all to look like so that others might be drawn into his kingdom.

Christ gives me his righteousness.

The gospel is the news that Christ lived a sinless life, was crucified in our place, and raised by the Spirit to conquer death for us after three days. But Christ's death does not make *us* righteous, rather it *imputes* Christ's righteousness to us (Rom. 4:5-8). You could think of it like a spiritual bank account into which Christ's righteousness is deposited in our name. It is from this account that payment is made for our sin. So when God looks at us, he sees the holy righteousness of his Son - the King.

Through Christ, we enter into a new covenant with God – a better way of relating to him that is not contingent on our performance or our position. But we know that God's story for the world doesn't end with the coming of the King nor the death of the King. There is still a lot left to the biblical story of restoration. Looking around, we still see pain and sorrow on earth.

And surely that is *not* the new kingdom of rest that God had in mind.

As we close the Gospels, we see that the story of Christ's work on our behalf is still unfinished. As Daughters of the King, we are dressed in his righteous garments and ready to enter the ball, but he is still making preparations for that royal celebration. As we wait for this final party, we will discover in the book of Acts that the King does something else for us that we might more fully enter into this new kingdom.

Chapter 7: The King Comes

1. Without peeking, can you name the five women mentioned by Matthew in the family tree of Jesus? (Matt. 1). What is notable about the inclusion of each of these women? Consider their origin, backstory, and role in the King's kingdom.

2. Review God's purpose in giving his people a temple in which to worship him.

3. According to John 1:14, Jesus replaces our need for a temple or tabernacle. What is the significance of this news for the King's daughters?

4. Daughters of the King go from being a slave to the Law of God to being freed from it. What role does the King play in our freedom?

As Daughters of the King, we live in light of the new covenant. Do you think it's easier to live in light of the old covenant sometimes? If yes, what are some common ways we live according to the old covenant?

CHAPTER 8: THE KING'S HELPER
ACTS

One of my kitchen drawers is trying to teach me grace. My dishtowel drawer has been a constant nuisance in my life for a while now.

It all started when I invited the twins to help me fold laundry. At the time I thought it was a stroke of genius, a real "win/win" for Team Mom. *The twins will improve their hand-eye coordination and fine motor skills, while I get a little assistance doing household chores*, I thought.

And after a few loads of laundry, I even patted my own back. *This is awesome*, I thought to myself. *I'm, like, the best mom ever – you know – teaching my kids skills they will use for the rest of their life.*

But after a few piles of laundry and one belligerent kitchen drawer later, I officially retracted all of my previous self-congratulations. You see, entrusting the laundry to Zach and Jonah requires me to do several things. And as you might have already guessed, these things don't come naturally to me.

First, entrusting the laundry to the twins means I must provide adequate and active supervision to the laundry-folding process. That means I must remain actively involved in the process offering a guiding hand and encouraging word while patiently watching the twins struggle over the dishtowels. No checking Facebook while the boys do the laundry. No sitting back sipping that third cup of coffee in the morning.

Second, entrusting the laundry to the twins means I must relinquish my desire to control the end result of the laundry-folding process. I know. That last one is a doozy. It convicted me even as I wrote it. Because, let's be honest, all you moms out there. It is easy to cheer your children on.

Offering kind words and sage counsel is one of those perks I believe God embedded in motherhood. Furthermore, it is easy to come to the aid of your children. What mom doesn't enjoy rescuing her children from harm's way?

But relinquishing control is a whole different matter. Those dishtowels I was telling you about? Yep. They're a mess. In fact, even as I write this there is a pile of them on my kitchen floor. I believe dishtowels should be folded neatly in the appropriate drawer and kept clean for future use. There is even a correct way to fold dishtowels. Oh, you didn't know that?

Believe me, it takes all the willpower I can muster to keep from re-folding the towels when the kids aren't looking. To do otherwise would be to clutch onto my desire for control a little too tightly. So, here's how my dishtowel drawer has been teaching me about grace.

Each time I open my dishtowel drawer, I'm reminded of the amazing grace shown to us each day by our loving and patient Father. The invitation to participate in the King's plan for redemptive history is nothing but a demonstration of his grace toward his daughters. Because like my laundry-folding sons, the King's daughters tend to work slowly. We tend to be high maintenance, requiring a lot of assistance and affirmation. We tend to whine and throw tantrums, particularly when circumstances don't turn out as we expected or desired. And ultimately, because we tend to leave messes in our wake.

How frustrating it must be for God to have billions of little human "helpers" running around his ankles. I mean, wouldn't it be easier to affect his will on earth all by himself? No doubt, it would. But by his grace, God allows us to participate in his plan to draw others to salvation (Eph. 2:10). And thankfully, in God's grace, he doesn't leave his daughters alone in this task. He gives us an important Helper to accomplish the task of being a Daughter of the King.

In chapter 7, we looked at the arrival of the promised King: Jesus Christ. We saw that Christ's arrival on earth was not enough to defeat evil and eradicate sin; he also had to die – die the death of humiliation, suffering, and judgment that should have been our fate. He did so as a perfect sacrifice, and in so doing, satisfied the righteous requirement of the Law and thereby God's wrath on all sinners.

As the four Gospels demonstrate, Christ's sinless life qualified him to serve as the perfect, eternal sacrifice for our sins.

In this chapter, our journey through the biblical story brings us to the book of Acts – the book immediately following the four Gospels. It is in the book of Acts that we learn Christ's death on earth is not the end of his story or the story of his followers; in fact, it is just the beginning.

Because after three days, Jesus was raised from the dead, conquering death due to sin once and for all (Rom. 6:4-11; 1 Cor. 15:3-4, 22-24, 55-56). By defeating death, Christ not only redeemed humanity from sin, but also redeems all creation from the effects of sin.

Through his resurrection, Christ ushers in (inaugurates) the new kingdom that the prophets spoke about. In short, all our hopes for complete, perfect, and total restoration are founded on Christ's resurrection.

THE KING INAUGURATES A NEW KINGDOM

Although we are going to spend the majority of our time in Acts in this chapter, I want to back up to the Gospel of Luke. The two books, Acts and Luke, stand as a pair. In fact, you could say that book of Luke is the prequel to the book of Acts.

Read Luke 24:1-27.

In Luke 24:1-27, we reach the climax in the biblical story: the gospel news of Christ's death and resurrection. Scripture repeatedly links the onset of God's new kingdom with the arrival of the promised King – Jesus Christ. So, when King Jesus conquers death by being raised to life, it is only natural for his disciples to wonder if the new, restored kingdom was at hand. This sentiment is spoken in Acts 1:6-7 when the disciples asked, *"Lord, will You at this time restore the kingdom to Israel?"*

But before the Creator completely restores his kingdom, a portion of his plan has yet to unfold. Christ repeatedly told his disciples that he desired all men to be saved and none to perish – a desire explicitly shared in the Old Testament (see chapter 8; Is. 49:4-6). In the book of Acts, those themes are highlighted all the more. And so, we see a delay between the inauguration of the kingdom and the final restoration of God's kingdom.

Listen up, Daughters of the King! This is the time in which we now live. The kingdom of God has begun, but it is not yet fully here. This is why many scholars describe the kingdom as both "now" and "not yet." Before ascending back into heaven, Christ promises the final kingdom and final restoration are still coming; they will occur when he returns to earth a second time. This anticipated event is called the second coming (Matt. 24:27, 30-31; Acts 1:9-11; 1 Thess. 4:16-17).

In the meantime, you and I live in a "now" and "not yet" kingdom. As believers, this is why we still have problems with sin despite Christ having already paid the penalty for our sin. This is why we still see injustices and suffering around us, even though Christ has ushered in a new type of world where wrong will one day be set right. This is why our relationships still fail and our bodies still break. The ugliness and consequences of sin will persist on earth until Christ comes again to finally, and totally, eradicate evil.

Yet, believers who have put their faith in Christ can still call themselves citizens of God's kingdom, even though they haven't witnessed or received the fullness of its blessings.[39]

In fact, it is imperative that we live our lives in a forward-looking fashion keeping a watchful and hopeful eye on our final restoration. Christ promised it was coming. For those who have already put their trust in Christ, we can be confident that God will fulfill that final promise of total restoration. We can be confident that life as we know it with all its brokenness and ugliness is not the end of our story as Daughters of the King!

THE KING COMMISSIONS HIS SUBJECTS

So what are we to do in the here and now, besides look forward to that final day of restoration?

Beginning in Genesis, and throughout the Old Testament, we've seen that God had a specific task for his people. As divine image bearers, they were to serve as his vice-regents over creation, representing God to all people. And in keeping with this same pattern, God has called all believers (citizens of his new kingdom) to a specific job as we await his second coming.

Read Luke 24:44-53.

In this passage, we see the scope of Christ's death. Christ died so all nations might hear his name and repent. God had his sights set on more than simply the restoration of his chosen people, Israel.

So, we see that through Christ's death and resurrection, all men – all nations – who repent are brought into a covenant relationship with God. And as such, they are given that special job in the kingdom to be a light to the nations. Christ will not come again until the good news of salvation is taken to all the nations. Matthew 24:14 says, *"And this gospel of the kingdom will be preached in all the world as a witness to all the nations, and then the end will come."*

Throughout the biblical story, we've noted that part of living under God's rule and enjoying his blessing was to fulfill the God-given role of being God's image bearers – to be his representatives on earth. Each one of us is a representative of God through Christ. Whether you are full-time minister or a servant in the pew, a mother of four or a single woman searching for God's best, the title of Daughter of the King is a resounding call to action. A true Daughter of the King spends little time sitting idly in the privileged position of the throne room. Instead, she is out among the people representing the goodness, humility, and submissive spirit of the One she serves. Emulating the actions of their King, who traded his glory for scorn and thorns, Daughters of the King eagerly exchange their gowns and crowns to do the precious and sometimes messy work of the gospel. Luckily, though, she's not alone.

THE KING SENDS A HELPER

As we said, despite inheriting Christ's righteousness, our transformation into a new creation has begun, but it is still not yet complete. While we are waiting for that final feasting day in that glorious kingdom, Christ promises to help us fulfill our role as his daughter.

Read Acts 1:1-8.

The book of Acts is a turning point in the history of God's people. Christ promises to send his Spirit - the Holy Spirit – to embolden believers, help guide us, convict us of sin in our own lives, and to equip us with spiritual gifts for this awesome task (cf. Rom. 8:9).

In fact, the rest of the book of Acts could very well be called the acts of the Holy Spirit, for it chronicles the lives of the apostles and the first believers as they placed their faith in Christ, were indwelt by the Holy Spirit, spread the news of salvation, and formed authentic communities of faith (churches) in their surrounding cities.

But I want to be clear. The Holy Spirit doesn't just 'appear' in the New Testament out of the blue. As a member of the triune Godhead, the Spirit is pre-existent along with the Father and the Son (Gen. 1; Job 33:4; Ps. 104:30). We greet him for the first time in Gen. 1:1 and hear the Godhead commune with each other in Gen. 1:26. Overall, the Old Testament features the Spirit in more subtle ways (Ps. 51:11, Isa. 63:11). But by the time we pick up the book of Luke, we've already seen the Spirit working in powerful, though often unseen, ways.[40]

This lesson is not intended to be an exhaustive teaching on the Spirit of God. Our perspective in this chapter falls in line with the way we've viewed all the books comprising the biblical story – to give a birds-eye view of the kingdom of God. So, let's look at some of the ways in which the Holy Spirit helped the early group of believers, and we'll see ways in which he continues to help us today as royal daughters with an important commission.[41]

The Holy Spirit brings new birth

In the book of Acts, the Spirit brings new birth. After Christ's ascension into heaven, the Father sends the Holy Spirit as promised (Acts 2). Immediately, the supernatural nature of the Spirit is seen. Some disbelieve Christ is the true King, and so Peter, by the power of the Spirit, boldly preaches concerning Christ. Incidentally, he preaches the unified story of the Scriptures drawing from the Law, Prophets, and the Writings.

Read Acts 2:37-39.

In Acts 2, we learn that the Holy Spirit is the one who convicts us of sin and directs us to the one Person qualified to fix our sin problem. The Holy Spirit points us to Christ. In Acts 2, it is only after hearing Peter's sermon about Jesus that the people were "cut to the heart" (Acts 2:37). They knew deep inside them there was a problem, and they were desperate to know how to fix it. With the help of the Spirit, Peter points them to Christ.

Can you identify with the people in Acts 2? Do you know there is a sin problem in your life – things are not the way they are supposed to be? Despite continually offering up your life – your deeds, your works – as a sacrifice to God, you know it is not enough. You know you need an eternal sacrifice for your sins. The Holy Spirit could be pricking your heart, pointing you to Christ, the only One capable of perfectly satisfying a holy God.

The Holy Spirit produces holiness

At conversion, believers receive the Holy Spirit (Rom. 8:9-11; 1 Cor. 3:16; 6:19, Eph. 1:13; 2 Tim. 1:14). In Acts 2, the gift of the indwelling of the Holy Spirit occurred after the people placed their trust in Christ. What proof do we have that God's Spirit was alive within the people? By the fruits that the Spirit produced in their lives. They were changed people.

Let's see what changes these people exhibited.

Read Acts 2:40-46.

These people exhibited a love for *God's Word*. Acts 2:42a says they were faithful to the Scriptures, correct doctrine, and spending time in prayer.[42] They also exhibited a love for their *brothers and sisters in Christ*. Acts 2:42b says they were faithful to fellowship with other believers by meeting physical and spiritual needs. And last, they exhibited a love for *serving others*. Acts 2:43-45 says they demonstrated signs and wonders that pointed people to Christ.

My husband and I recently transplanted from Texas to Pennsylvania. Shortly after arriving, God led us to join the core group of a new church. In fact, when we signed on at Living Faith Community Church, it had yet to hold its first official worship service as a church. We spent the majority of our pre-launch phase forming our core group, delving deeply into Acts 2 and the characteristics demonstrated by the early church. We saw, above all, that the Spirit is the one engendering holiness and fellowship among us. As much as we would like to say that we planted Living Faith Community Church, we know it is the Spirit's role to produce an authentic community of faith among us and grow it to maturation.

In the same way, the Spirit's mark among the early believers in Acts 2 is unmistakable. These people were being transformed into the image of Christ by demonstrating to others the love Christ first showed to them. They were being progressively transformed into Christ's holy image by the Spirit.

Those of us who already have a relationship with God (consider ourselves God's people, living in God's place, and submitting to his rule) should be demonstrating the fruits of the Spirit in our everyday thoughts and deeds. This fruit is evidence that we have placed our trust in him and depend on his Spirit to produce holiness in our lives.

We must learn to listen to the Spirit's guiding as he seeks to transform us. In one of the Bible studies I attended, my discussion group said we would love for holiness to be our 'default' reaction to life. By that we meant that often it is hard to do the right thing. It is much easier to do the wrong thing. It's easy to snap at others when we're tired or sick. It's hard to be patient and loving. It's easy to gossip. It's hard to hold our tongues and speak words of peace. It's easy to punish others when we don't get our way by being in a bad mood, giving others the ol' silent treatment, or 'writing them off our list.' (Don't act like you don't know what I mean!)

It's hard to be gracious. It's difficult to trust and wait on the Lord. It's much easier to despair, throw ourselves a giant pity party, and let anxious thoughts about the future hold us hostage in the present.

We're speaking much about actions the early church undertook – they studied the Scripture, they shared themselves, they served others. All of these things are impossible without the Holy Spirit. He is the one who helps us, guides us, counsels us, teaches us, shapes us into the image of Christ (John 14:15-26; Rom. 8:14, 26). Even after Christ's resurrection and the gift of the Holy Spirit, we still have a sin problem. It hasn't been eradicated 100 percent, right?

So, don't be discouraged if your transformation into Christ's image seems slow – or slower than those around you. It is a process. And when Christ comes again, the Spirit will complete his work in our lives as our restoration is finally fulfilled.

First John 3:1-3 is one of my favorite verses of all time. It speaks to the promise of finality: *"Behold what manner of love the Father has bestowed on us, that we should be called children of God! Therefore the world does not know us, because it did not know Him. Beloved, now we are children of God; and it has not yet been revealed what we shall be, but we know that when He is revealed, we shall be like Him, for we shall see Him as He is. And everyone who has this hope in Him purifies himself, just as He is pure."*

The Holy Spirit equips us for service

In the same way the Holy Spirit gives us new birth and purifies us, he also equips us for service. Luke, as the author of Acts, uses the terminology of 'witnesses.'

Read Acts 4:1-4, 13, 23-31.

The Holy Spirit equips us for service by making us bold. The Holy Spirit emboldened the people of God so they could fulfill his call to make disciples of all nations. In this passage, Peter has just been arrested for being so bold as to preach the gospel in the temple to the Jews! Before the Holy Spirit came, the very same Peter denied even knowing Christ. But after receiving the Holy Spirit, he is bold enough to preach to hundreds at a time and even preach in the most dangerous locations.

The Holy Spirit equips us for service by giving us unique gifts. The Spirit also equips us so we might serve one another in the church. Scripture is clear that through the Holy Spirit, each of us receives a special gift after we've placed our trust in Christ. Throughout the book of Acts, we see various men and women serving in different capacities. Joanna and Susanna, women healed by Jesus, were generous givers (Luke 8:1-3). The woman at the well was an evangelist (John 4:28-30). Lydia opened her home (Acts 16:40). Phoebe served (Rom. 16:1). Priscilla taught (Acts 18:26). The point is, the King's gifts and purpose are as unique as each of his daughters.

First Cor. 12:7 speaks clearly regarding these spiritual gifts: *"But the manifestation of the Spirit is given to each one for the profit of all…"* You can read the entire chapter of 1 Cor. 12 to learn more about them, but I want to point you toward this underlying message – each gift is special because it is given by the Holy Spirit. More importantly, however, is the purpose for which each gift is portioned – for the benefit of the community of faith.

The task of being a vice-regent is difficult, and it takes faith. Has God ever called you to do something that you are scared to do? Scripture is replete with examples of both men and women who doubted they could fulfill the responsibility God called them to.

I can't help but think of Moses who was too afraid to speak to Pharaoh or Jeremiah who thought he was too young to be a prophet. I think of Sarah who believed herself too old to bear the child promised to her husband. The list goes on and on! God doesn't call you to serve him and then leave you on your own to figure it out. Rather, God promises to equip you for the job he's called you to do, and the Holy Spirit does just that.

As his daughter, he will make you bold like Moses. He will give you wisdom like Jeremiah. He will give you strength like Sarah. Through the Holy Spirit, the King gives his daughters a supernatural gift to accomplish our task. Moses, Jeremiah, and Sarah all attest that the Spirit works in our weaknesses to display God's strength. Maybe Moses really was a bad speaker, and maybe Jeremiah really was too young to be taken seriously. Truly, Sarah was too old to cultivate life inside her. The point is, the very area of your life you consider to be a deficiency is often the area in which God's glory shines the brightest.

CONCLUSION

Israel, although greatly favored by God in their covenant relationship, struggled greatly to fulfill their role to be a light to the nations. Christ, as the Ultimate Light, shows us how to live and calls us to live in his likeness – to be a light much like Israel was intended to be.

While we live in the kingdom that is both "now" and "not yet," we still see

God's promises at play. Let's review and see how the inauguration of the new kingdom and the help of the Holy Spirit impacts each of these promises to us today as Daughters of the King.

God's People

In the Old Testament, the people of God included those who had entered into a covenant with the King, namely, Israel. Yet even under the old covenant, God's desire to restore all nations was clear.[43] But with the coming of Christ to earth as the one true Light, the old covenant was fulfilled and a new covenant was introduced. And while the church in no way replaces Israel, the two groups – both the faithful Jew and Gentile who have surrendered to Christ – comprise the body of God's people (Rom. 11; Eph. 3:1-9). Today, all believers are brought into the covenant of God and given the special task to be a light to the nations and draw others to Christ.

First Peter 2:9, written to a Gentile audience, summarizes this hope: *"But you are a chosen generation, a royal priesthood, a holy nation, His own special people, that you may proclaim the praises of Him who called you out of darkness into His marvelous light."* The title that once belonged only to Abraham and his seed now describes all those who trust in Christ for salvation. Being a Daughter of the King means you are a descendant of Abraham and part of the people of God by virtue of your relationship to the Son.

God's Place

In our earlier studies, we noted the importance of land to Israel as a symbol of both God's kingdom and his presence with man. We saw in chapter 7 that Jesus Christ became the 'land' for God's people, functioning as the true temple of God. And when Christ sends his Helper to indwell his sons and daughters, God's very own people become his temple. That is why in 1 Peter 2:9 Peter uses terms like "holy," calling believers to live a holy life (cf. Eph. 2:20-21; 1 Cor. 6:19-20).

God's Rule and Blessing

Having been set free from the judgment of sin and clothed in Christ's righteousness, we, as Daughters of the King, can now enjoy the blessings of the new covenant.[44] With the presence of the Holy Spirit to convict us, guide us, and equip us for service, we have all the tools to help us "live up to God's standards" and fulfill our task to be priests to the nations.[45] It is now possible for us to live under the rule of the King and in the kingdom of God. That is not to say it's easy since the kingdom is both now and not yet.

God's People	God's Place	God's Rule & Blessing
All those who trust in God's Son THE CHURCH (believing Jews & Gentiles)	All those indwelt with God's Spirit THE CHURCH (individuals and the church)	All those living in obedience to God's Word THE CHURCH (with the Spirit's help)

My Story:

I must live my life looking forward to my ultimate restoration.

Above all things, I hope you'll remember that the age in which you live is an "inbetween" time. This present age is not the end of the biblical story. And the circumstances in which you find yourself - abandoned by a loved one, battling illnesses, or carrying around financial regret – are not the final chapters in your story as a Daughter of the King.

The biblical story tells us that Christ is coming again, and when he does so, the King's daughters will be completely and perfectly restored along with the entire earth. In the meantime, the Holy Spirit in us gives us a foretaste of what the new creation will be like and what our lives will look like. Romans 8:23 says, *"Not only that, but we also who have the firstfruits of the Spirit, even we ourselves groan within ourselves, eagerly waiting for the adoption, the redemption of our body."*

Paul says we have the "firstfruits" of the Spirit, meaning the part of the Holy Spirit that resides in us today will be magnified even more at the end. Today, the King gives his daughters a small measure, but tomorrow we will reap the full harvest of blessings of the restored kingdom.

This is our hope: that God will totally restore us and the entire earth from sin. Life as we know it (with all its pain and suffering) is not the end of our story! Because it is not the end of Christ's!

I must live as a light drawing others to Christ.

As a divine image bearer, you are called to a special task as vice-regent over

God's creation. The title of a Daughter of the King means more than a posh residence and special access to the throne. The title of the Daughter of the King comes with the awesome responsibility to be a light, representing God to the nations so that others might be drawn to the King.

This role as an image-bearer and sub-regent is the most difficult challenge we will face in our walk with Christ. It is easy to speak well of the King to others when circumstances are running in our favor. It is easy to boast in the King's affections when we are blessed financially, emotionally, and more. But it not so easy to be bold in proclaiming the greatness of the King's kingdom when we are barely making ends meet, shouldering a debilitating illness, or plowed over by a broken marriage. Our role as a light can seem quite counter-intuitive when the "now" of the Kingdom seems threadbare and dull.

But do not let your eyes deceive your hearts, because as we learned in chapter 4, God delights in using broken vessels through which to showcase his glory. True Daughters of the King speak well of their King even when daily life has lost its gleam.

I trust God will equip me for service through his Spirit.

The same God who commissions us as his daughters will not leave us to uphold our task alone. He provides the life, boldness, and equipping to carry out the sometimes challenging but always rewarding job as a sub-regent, particularly when we have nothing within us to spend on others. We can be fearless in our pursuit of the role God has given us, knowing that his Spirit goes before us and produces life and growth.

The same Spirit that testifies that we are, in fact, related to the King will equip us to fulfill our task in the King's kingdom.

Chapter 8: The King's Helper

1. What is the 'now' and 'not yet' reality of the King's kingdom?

2. What does the 'now' and 'not yet' kingdom mean for me as a Daughter of the King?

3. Daughters of the King bear the King's image in who they are and what they do. When we act as a representative of the King, we "image" God to others. When others see you, do you think they see a royal princess sitting pretty or an active and gracious servant

of the throne?

4. Thankfully, God helps us fulfill our roles as his daughter. What are the three ways mentioned in this chapter that the Helper assists the King's daughters?

When we look forward to our final restoration, we are viewing life with "kingdom eyes." What circumstances are you currently walking in that could use "kingdom eyesight"? How can your circumstance(s) be used as a light to draw others to the King?

CHAPTER 9: THE KING'S PRIESTS
THE EPISTLES

The market was poorly lit, a fact I didn't mind since it concealed the layers of dirt and grime coating every surface I was touching. As we wound through the maze of furniture stalls, squeezing over chairs and chests stacked 7-feet high, a man with a wide grin approached us. He peeked out at us through greasy bangs and said he wanted to help us find the perfect piece of furniture. But we quickly discovered he owned no shop among the hundreds of booths set up in the large building. He was a bonafide middle man, helping foreigners who didn't speak the local language get the "very best price" for their purchases.

My husband and I quickly assessed the situation. There were a few advantages to using a middle man. Bargaining for a wooden trunk might be hard since we didn't speak the language. Plus, the man seemed intimately acquainted with every shop owner, having already worked out a system for pricing and shipping. Indeed, much of the legwork had already been done.

But we also knew a middle man came with inherent disadvantages. With another person in the mix, we wouldn't be getting the cheapest deal. The middle man would receive a portion of our purchase price, a factor the shop owner had likely already calculated into the cost of the furniture. With a middle man, we wouldn't be able to speak to the shop owner directly. We wouldn't get to hear the history of our piece directly from him. And I wanted to know who made the trunk, what materials he used, what village it came from, and how to care for it. Using a middle man would mean I would have to be content with hearing all those details through our translator and trust that all the information was conveyed and conveyed accurately.

Every culture is familiar with the concept of a middle man - a mediator.

These mediators pop up everywhere from Vietnamese fishing villages to New York's Wall Street. It's a concept with incredibly ancient roots. The idea of a middle man or mediator appears very early in the Scriptures. It was (and still is) an important role with huge implications for daily life.

You and I became Daughters of the King solely because of a middle man, a mediator. The King we serve acted in this way, inviting us into the Father's throne room based on his royal status. We are tapped as an heir to the throne, not because of gifts, talents, or good behavior, but because the King gave us royal clothing to wear and adopted us into his royal family (Is. 61:10). We are made Daughters of the King based on the activity of the King.

In this chapter, we will look at the **Epistles**, the letters of the New Testament, and what they have to say about the role of a mediator. But first, turn to the table of contents in your Bible and look at where these letters fall in the biblical story. During our time together, we've been looking at God's story for the world, and where our lives fit into that story.

We began with the **Law** (the first five books of the Bible), where we discovered God established a restful pattern for our lives in which man acted as the King's sub-regents on earth. This is God's plan for his kingdom. Remember our definition of the kingdom? God's people living in God's place under God's rule and blessing. And even though sin disrupted that pattern, it didn't mean God tossed his plan out the window. Rather he set about to restore both man and all creation to its original state.

And God continued to use his good pattern of including mankind in his kingdom, of allowing his daughters to participate with God in his plan of salvation. We saw this in the **History Books** (Joshua – Esther) and in **the Writings and the Prophets** (Isaiah – Malachi). In these sections, we learned that Israel was called to be a blessing to the nations (Gen. 12). More specifically, they were called to be a holy priesthood (Ex. 19:6),a nation set apart, so that when other pagan nations looked at them and observed their holy, unique life they would be drawn into a covenant relationship with God. Their submission to the rule of the King was not just for their own good, but so that their lives might stand as a light to the unbelieving nations surrounding them (Exod. 19:5-6; Deut. 4:20; 7:6; Isa. 43:20-1).

Then we entered into the New Testament with the **Gospels** (Matthew - John) and discovered the good news: The much-anticipated restoration of all the King's subjects and his kingdom begins with the death and resurrection of Jesus Christ, the Son of God. As the perfect and final mediator, Jesus literally acted as our middle man, giving his daughters unhindered access to the throne of God. In the book of **Acts** we learned that Jesus sent a Helper to the earth (the Holy Spirit) to encourage and equip us in our calling as his sub-regents.

Now it's time for us to get a birds-eye view of the **Epistles**, letters written by the apostles to the early believers in the years following Christ's resurrection. These 21 letters (Romans – Jude) were written mostly to the churches that began to spring up as a result of the witness of the apostles and early followers of Christ. These letters are written to both Jews and non-Jews living in many different cities and cultures. Primarily, the apostles were concerned that these believers fulfill their role as a light to the nations.

The Epistles tell us, as Daughters of the King, that we carry out this similar role. Just as ancient Israel was both sub-regent and a middle man to the surrounding nations, we, too, are called to be a light to the nations.

In fact, did you know that the Bible calls you a priest? If you are part of the covenant community of Christ – redeemed from sin by him and have placed your trust in him – then you are considered a priest. Sounds kind of weird, doesn't it? Because most of the time we feel anything but holy. Anything but honorable. Anything but spiritual. Let's be honest. Sometimes it's easier for me to view myself as a royal than a priest; there are some days when my actions and my heart attitude are anything but pure.

But even while we live under the new covenant of Christ, we still see that God's purposes for our relationship remain the same. Just like Israel, our relationship with God through Christ is not just for our own good (our own salvation), but so our lives might stand as a light to the unbelievers surrounding us. And while we do not replace ancient Israel, like them we serve as a kingdom of priests today.[46]

THE ROLE OF THE KING'S PRIESTS

A Representative of the People

Have you ever thought of yourself as a priest? Chances are, no! Because we still battle with sin and its devastating effects, we often feel the furthest thing from a holy person whose life is set apart to draw others into a covenant relationship with Christ.

> **Definition: Priest**: A representative of the people to God. "Personnel

in charge of sacrifice and offerings at worship places, particularly the tabernacle and temple."[47]

Significance: Priests were representatives of the people to God. They mediated God's Word and work to God's people.

As an official duty in ancient Israel, God gave Moses instructions to ordain Aaron and his four sons as priests "to serve at the altar and in the sanctuary" (Ex. 28:1, 41). Later, the tribe of Levi was given priestly duties (Ex. 40:13, Num. 1:47-54). The priests acted as a representative on behalf of the people to bring resolution to the people's relationship with God. The significance of the priesthood is seen most clearly on the Day of Atonement, one day a year in which the High Priest would enter the holiest place in the temple, the Holy of Holies, and offer a sacrifice on behalf of all the people. But this system was imperfect because each year a new sacrifice was needed.

In the New Testament, this representative role is fulfilled by Christ. He is our mediator, or "middle man," between a sinful people and a holy God.

Read Hebrews 4:14-16; 9:11-15.

The author of Hebrews tells us Christ is the better High Priest. Through the shedding of his innocent blood on our behalf, he becomes not just the perfect High Priest, but the perfect sacrifice as well. We have already talked about the significance of Christ's sacrifice – that it was an eternal sacrifice securing for us eternal redemption.[48] But in his priestly duties, Christ acted as the middle man, the mediator, representing us to God. And because he is eternal, his activity as an effective mediator is eternal as well. As a result, man and God may dwell directly and intimately together forever!

Since Scripture is clear that Christ's work as a priest on our behalf is finished, completed, eternal, there is no longer any need for additional sacrifices. Likewise, Christ eternally represents us to the Father. So, there is no longer a need for any other human mediators between man and God. Christ is our eternal mediator. It's why the author of Hebrews says that we can approach the "throne of grace" and God himself with great boldness (Heb. 4:16). As Daughters of the King, no more barriers exist in our relationship with our Father; you and I have unhindered access to the King.

A Redeemed Life

Despite having a final and eternal mediator, Scripture still calls all of us as his daughters to be a holy priesthood of believers.

Read 1 Peter 2:5-9.

Written by Peter just prior to the persecutions of Roman Emperor Nero (64 A.D.), the letters of 1 & 2 Peter are set during a time of great danger for believers. Peter wrote these two letters to encourage believers in Christ-like living despite the dangerous times. He encourages them by reminding them of their future hope.

Key to this passage is verse 9. What is God's purpose in calling us a holy nation, a royal priesthood? *"…that you may proclaim the praises of Him who called you out of darkness into His marvelous light."*

As priests, we are to draw others to Christ. We no longer do this by representing the people to the Father (because Christ does that for us eternally), but by serving and ministering in other ways – by praying for one another, by doing good works, and by encouraging one another in living holy lives.[49] I like how Paul puts it in Rom. 12:1: *"I beseech you therefore, brethren, by the mercies of God, that you present your bodies a living sacrifice, holy, acceptable to God, which is your reasonable service."* As priests, we are to present our lives as a living sacrifice, mirroring the selfless sacrifice of Christ on the cross (cf. Phil. 4:18). As a "body" of priests, our ministry occurs within the context of other believers - a corporate ministry of the church.[50]

Probably the most difficult aspect of the title of Daughter of the King is ensuring the way we live matches up with the holy King we serve. The way we live matters. The way we respond to others matters. We have been set apart for an important task – to draw others out of darkness into his marvelous light.

As a mother, the way I live at home with my family matters. If my heart is focused on the King, my words and ways will be characterized by his light and love. If my heart is focused on myself, then you can imagine what other things will tumble out of my mouth. Hebrews 13:15 says, *"Therefore by Him let us continually offer the sacrifice of praise to God, that is, the fruit of our lips, giving thanks to His name."*

The gospel requires me to ask myself, *what do my children hear spilling from my lips the most often?* Praise and gratitude or anger and frustration? When my children see anxiety on my face and hear fear in my words, I am not drawing them into the marvelous light of Christ. Instead, I'm steering them toward darkness.

As a team player in the office are my words uplifting or do I spend time grumbling about others and with others? When my co-worker watches me respond to injustices or slights with angry or even sarcastic words, I am not encouraging them to plunge the depths of their own heart in order to see their need for a Savior. I am encouraging them to savor the darkness. The way we live as the King's daughters matters. Thankfully, this task is not endeavored alone; we have the King's Spirit to aid us.

THE REWARD OF THE KING'S PRIESTS – AN ETERNAL INHERITANCE

Today, God's pattern of calling his people to be a holy priesthood still rings true, only the participants have changed. God has widened his covenant to all believers. And while Israel remains God's chosen people, all who demonstrate faith and trust in Christ are given the spiritual blessings of Abraham. Scripture calls all those who believe in Christ the sons of Abraham, and as such, are promised to receive an inheritance.

The idea of inheritance is especially moving for women. In the Ancient Near East, the lines of inheritance fell to the eldest son. For the Israelites, inheritances kept divisions of land in their family; it is how they held onto the promises of God. Yet, even in the Old Testament we see the idea of inheritance widened to a spiritual significance. All the tribes of Israel were given land, except one: the tribe of the Levi. Scripture notes the Lord himself was the inheritance of the Levites (Num. 18:20-24; Deut. 10:9; 18:2; Josh. 13:33). Similarly, Israel itself is called the 'inheritance' of the Lord (Jer. 10:16).

So by the time we get to the New Testament, inheritance can mean property, but it "most often refers to rewards of discipleship." These rewards include *eternal life* (Matt. 5:5, 19:29; Mark 10:29-30; Titus 3:4-7) and the *kingdom* itself (Matt. 25:34; James 2:5; 1 Cor. 6:9-10; 15:50).[51]

I like how Matthew 25:31-34 puts it: *"When the Son of Man comes in His glory, and all the holy angels with Him, then He will sit on the throne of His glory. All the nations will be gathered before Him, and He will separate them one from another, as a shepherd divides his sheep from the goats. And He will set the sheep on His right hand, but the goats on the left. Then the King will say to those on His right hand, 'Come, you blessed of My Father, inherit the kingdom prepared for you from the foundation of the world.'"*

Through Christ, Christians are heirs of God's kingdom. All those who place their trust in Christ are called "co-heirs" with Christ (Rom. 8:17; Eph. 3:6).

Rom. 8:14-17 says, *"For as many as are led by the Spirit of God, <u>these are sons of God</u>. For you did not receive the spirit of bondage again to fear, but you received the Spirit of adoption by whom we cry out, "Abba, Father." The Spirit himself bears witness with our spirit that we are children of God, <u>and if children, then heirs</u>—heirs of God and joint heirs with Christ, if indeed we suffer with Him, that we may also be glorified together."*[52]

When Christ inaugurated the new kingdom, he inaugurated our eternal inheritance in him. (Heb. 9:16-17). So, as a priest and his daughter, you and I are slated to receive and co-rule the kingdom with Christ. Do you see how God's pattern for life continues even today? Adam and Eve were meant to be sub-rulers over the earth under God's rule. But today, you and I (if we trust in Christ) are Daughters of the King and are named priests and co-rulers with Christ over his new kingdom.

Being a Daughter of the King speaks not only to what we'll gain in the end and where we'll sit, but it also speaks to the loving way God views each of his daughters. Far from being a contractual relationship, Ephesians 1 tells us that God considers each of us *his* inheritance as well. In Eph. 1:18, Paul prays that the Ephesian believers might truly understand *"the hope of His calling, what are <u>the riches of the glory of His inheritance</u> in the saints..."*

We are God's portion, his inheritance, and stand as "his most treasured possession."[53] This speaks of the "extraordinary value he places on us."[54] Through our relationship with him, God displays the riches of his love and glory. He is invested in our lives, and when people see our walk, they will (and should) see God's great love.

This idea of God's people being his inheritance didn't start in the New Testament. Paul is speaking out of a knowledge steeped in Old Testament theology. In Genesis, God's people are known as the sons of God. And Moses sets up a case for God being faithful to his promises to preserve his people, so that they *can* be God's inheritance (Deut. 32:9).

In Exodus, God saves the people out of slavery for one purpose: to *be* his inheritance (Ex. 19). In the Law, the fact that we are God's inheritance is tied up with receiving an inheritance in the Land.

And this is the key: we cannot inherit what we are promised (eternal life) unless God inherits us first. And it does nothing for God's glory to inherit a broken canvas that was once lovely but is now torn by sin. The biblical story is indeed a love story; the story of how the King loved his daughters so much that he restored us to the glory in which we once stood.

THE KING'S PROMISES PARTIALLY FULFILLED

The Epistles tell us how to live in the present in light of our salvation as a priesthood of believers. But these letters also tell us what we can expect in the future as Christ's priests – an *eternal inheritance.*

And so we can see the ultimate restoration of God's kingdom getting closer and closer. The King is on his throne. The King's Helper - his Spirit - is actively working through us and for us on the earth. And the King's co-heirs and co-rulers are acting as priests in order to bring others into the kingdom and prepare for the King's second arrival.

So, let's look at those promises given first to Abraham and see how they relate to us today as Christ's priests and his daughters.

God's People

The title of God's people now extends to all who repent of their sins and place their trust in Christ for salvation. This includes both the Jew and the Gentile (non-Jew), encompassing all nations (Is. 42:6; 49:6). Through Christ it is possible for people of any tribe, tongue, culture, and nation to enter into a covenant relationship with God. If we are found in Christ, we are all sons and daughters of the King. And all those who have this relationship with God through Christ are given the task of priests and are heirs of the restored kingdom.

God's Place

In chapter 8, we learned that the Holy Spirit further fulfills the promise given to Abraham of land, a place to dwell with God. Once a person repents of sin and places their trust in Christ, they are "indwelt" with the Holy Spirit, the Helper who empowers us to share about Christ, purifies us from sin, and equips us to serve as his priests. We no longer need a physical place to dwell with God. Rather we, as his priests, become the spiritual dwelling place of God. This is true in the lives of individual believers as well as in the life of the church.

God's Rule and Blessing

As priests and co-heirs of the King's kingdom, believers are securely fitted under God's rule. Although the writers of the Epistles still call believers to obey God's commandments, we are no longer slaves to the Law. Christ, as the sinless sacrifice, perfectly fulfilled the "righteous requirement of the Law" on our behalf. Now, it is through Christ that we receive the blessings of dwelling intimately and directly with the King and being under his rule. For those in a covenant relationship with God, those blessings are an "eternal inheritance" and cannot be taken away. Furthermore, Christ gave us His Spirit to aid us in obedience.

The blessings of an "eternal inheritance" come only with a relationship with God through Christ. You can know about God and believe he exists and still not receive those precious blessings. The blessings come only through a relationship, being counted as his.

Do you have a covenant relationship with Christ? Entering into that covenant is as simple as repenting for your sin and trusting in him.

"Then Peter said to them, 'Repent, and let every one of you be baptized in the name of Jesus Christ for the remission of sins; and you shall receive the gift of the Holy Spirit.'" Acts 2:38

CONCLUSION

Even with the partial fulfillment of these covenant promises, we still see that the kingdom is imperfect.

Even as we are claimed by God as his people, we still sin. We still see sin around us and are heavily impacted by the sins of others. Even as we are given the Holy Spirit as a helper, we still are not totally restored to the immediate presence of God. Rather, the Holy Spirit in our lives is meant as a "foretaste" of what our lives will be like when we dwell directly in the presence of the Creator himself. And even as we are living under the King's rule and experiencing the blessings wrought by Christ today, we are promised an "eternal inheritance" in the near future – an inheritance that involves co-rulership with Christ himself!

Our introduction into the covenant community of Christ is not the end of God's story. Our role as priests in this age is not the final act in ours either. An even greater kingdom and priesthood is coming – one perfectly restored to its original goodness. We'll read about that in the next chapter.

My Story:

I am co-heir with Christ of God's kingdom.

All those that place their trust in Christ are called "co-heirs" with Christ (Rom. 8:17; Eph. 3:6). Being an heir and heiress comes as a natural result of our relationship with the King.

A few years ago, my friend, Sara, took in two foster daughters in an emergency situation. Her courageous actions brought her already full house to five kids ages 4, 11, 13, 14, and 16. Struggling to meet the needs of each child, feed four perpetually hungry teens, help transition the foster daughters into an emotionally-healthy environment, work a full-time job, and still be a witness to her family and community seemed an impossible task.

Yet, God has proven himself to be at work in her life despite the onset of poor circumstances that followed her decision – loss of paychecks, extra bills, family conflict, housing drama, and more. Her choice was not only the kindest thing she could have done for her foster daughters, it also proved to be the wisest thing she could have done for her family. In inviting those two girls into her home, Sara and her husband painted a vivid portrait of the Father's love for his children as he invites us as strangers into his dwelling place and gives us a permanent and prominent place at his table.

I am called to draw others to Christ in my daily life.

The way we live matters. The way we respond to others matters. We have been set apart for an important task – to draw others out of darkness into his marvelous light.

When my friend, Sara, opened her home and heart to two foster daughters, she provided them with a shining example of how the Father relates to us. He rescues us, invites us into his royal family, and gives us special purpose and meaning as co-heirs of his kingdom. In adopting us as his own, the Father redeems our terrible circumstances – some of our own making, some not – and turns our histories into stories for his glory. He gives his daughters a lavish home to which we are unaccustomed, an unbreakable family, a place of security and belonging, an unshakeable self-worth, a new name, a new purpose, ample provisions, and eternal blessings of love.

A few months ago, my friend's foster daughters became her own. She threw a huge bash to celebrate their adoption into her family. And that day, we celebrated more than a piece of paper confirming their new legal status or potential avenues of inheritance later in life. We celebrated their identity as members of a family of faith. The light of the kingdom shone brilliantly from her house that day, as many friends, neighbors, and acquaintances squeezed into every room of her house.

The way we live matters. The way we respond to needs around us matters. And while our actions do not garner us any special privileges with the King, when we are obedient to do as he asks, he uses our actions to speak of the gracious love he has poured into our lives.

I am given an "eternal inheritance" in my relationship with Christ.

As a Daughter of the King, we are promised special blessings. But these blessings of an "eternal inheritance" come only through our relationship with Jesus Christ, our King.

When my friend adopted her foster daughters, no longer did they simply occupy a temporary bed in her house and accept some of the perks of living in their home like food, lodging, or protection from the elements. They became part of her family. They received a new name. They received a new future. And while they continue to work through and let go of some of their past, they can do so knowing that their future is not contingent or tainted by what happened to them or what they did yesterday, last month, or last year. Their place in her new home and family is secure.

That's what God does for us as his daughters. He rescues us from our pits. And instead of just letting us shelter in his house until the storm passes and offering us a few plates of food from his table, he adopts us into his family. We become his. We bear his name. We are given a future that is eternally secure. And in the end, he's throwing us a huge adoption celebration, a marvelous banquet that, although it's hard for me to fathom, just might out do the table at my friend's house.

As Daughters of the King, we become an heir to the King's kingdom. We are given the blessings of salvation and his righteousness. We are tasked to act as a priest to those around us, showcasing the love of the King for all those who desire to enter his home.

Chapter 9: The King's Priests

1. How do we become a Daughter of the King, restored to our role as a representation and representative of the King? Did you have anything to do with your royal title and position?

2. Turn to the Table of Contents in your Bible. What does each section of the biblical story we've studied so far say about your identity as a

Daughter of the King? (Hint: Review the conclusion of each chapter and the 'My Story' sections).

3. How is Christ the better High Priest? (See Heb. 4:14-16; 9:11-15). What is the significance of having Jesus Christ as our permanent and eternal priest?

4. If Christ is the perfect, final High Priest, then why do the Epistles tell us that the King's daughters are also priests? (See 1 Pet. 2:5-9).

Being a Daughter of the King speaks not only to what we'll gain in the end (a royal inheritance) and where we'll sit (by our King!) but also to the loving way God views each of his daughters. Are you secure in the belief that God loves you, or do you rate God's feelings for you according to your circumstances?

LESSON 10: THE KINGDOM AT REST
REVELATION

Steve and Susan Vinton moved to Tanzania about five years ago, but they didn't intend on staying. Their home was the Congo. They were missionaries there but were forced to leave for political reasons. So, they sought a temporary haven in Tanzania. But the couple soon discovered something that compelled them to stay. They found village after village of children who would never go to school. They found village after village of people dying of a mysterious illness. They found village after village hungry in need of the Bread of Life. And so the Vinton family stayed in Tanzania to fulfill their call to be "priests" to all nations. And since that time, God has worked mightily through this family, drawing many into the marvelous light of the King's kingdom (1 Pet. 2).[55]

Today, the Vintons partner with villages in Tanzania and neighboring Malawi, teaching the villagers how to raise their own supplies and build their own school as a community. Then through their organization, Village Schools International, the Vintons supply missionary teachers for the schools. In less than ten years, they have seen 188 villages work together to open 26 schools. Another eight are currently under construction. The organization's website reports that, as of 2013, over 8,300 students are now working toward an education who otherwise would have never gone to school.

But Susan found that the lack of access to education was not the only barrier for these communities. As they spent time with the people, she encountered village after village with a then unnamed illness: AIDS. Today, Susan ferries almost 1,000 sick women and children to a hospital that is about 2.5 hours away by a bus she purchased so they can get much-needed medicine.

The Vintons are literally transforming lives, demonstrating and sharing the love of God's kingdom with all nations. The Vintons are living, breathing priests on earth. In the last chapter, we looked at what it means to be a priest: Someone who has placed their faith in Christ is transformed into a priest of the gospel. As Daughters of the King, our function, much like ancient Israel, is to be a holy people set apart for Christ and his kingdom, guiding all nations to worship the King.

We also learned that Christ is our final High Priest, and it is after the life of this holy, sinless Servant King that we are to arrange our lives. As the King's daughters, we have been given an unshakeable eternal inheritance – one day we will co-rule over his kingdom with him forever!

Although we have been given a foretaste of this eternal inheritance through the Holy Spirit in our lives, we will not receive the fullness of these blessings until all creation is restored to fellowship with God. Right now we live between two ages – between the two advents of Christ. So, we see the importance of the present for drawing the nations to Christ through our royal and priestly service – a challenging role we can only fulfill with the Spirit's help. Yet, it is the future on which we set our hopes, knowing that a new creation is coming. Our final restoration as a royal daughter in the King's court is coming.

In this final chapter, we will look at that final restoration as recorded in the book of Revelation. Revelation is the last book in the Bible and chronicles the culmination of God's plan to restore all creation. The apostle John wrote this book while in exile (around AD 81-96) to seven churches located in modern-day Turkey. These churches were greatly persecuted under the Roman Emperor Domitian (Rev. 2:10, 13). Revelation is written in an unusual style which often makes for difficulty in reading and interpretation. By genre it is called apocalyptic literature and is characterized by great symbolism.[56]

At the time the book was written, its original readers would have found great joy in its words and imagery because of the great hope which they conveyed. John tells them that he has seen a vision of how life would end for them. Their lives would not end in the suffering they were immediately experiencing, but instead Christ would put a stop to their suffering – forever! This is the message the Vintons carry to Tanzania – that all the promises of God made to Abraham and to us as co-rulers with Christ would finally be fulfilled![57] That any individual who trusts in God's promises regarding his Son, the King, can be made a son or daughter in his court.

THE KING RETURNS

So, let's look at how the final restoration will unfold in the biblical story and what it means for the story of the King's daughters.

The King Takes His Throne

The book of Revelation tells us that God gives the apostle John a series of visions. One vision gives us a glimpse of the return of the King. It's a vision of a sacrificial Lamb claiming his throne.

Read Revelation 4.

Many good, trustworthy scholars are divided on the meaning of the symbolism behind this passage. My point here is not to try to discern the identity of the impressive creatures or the 24 elders, but to highlight their activity. What are they doing? They are engaged in worship. And what does their worship look like? In verses 10-11, we're given a description: *"the twenty-four elders fall down before Him who sits on the throne and worship Him who lives forever and ever, and cast their crowns before the throne, saying: 'You are worthy, O Lord, To receive glory and honor and power; For You created all things, And by Your will they exist and were created.'"*

The elders, who are royal (wearing golden crowns), are casting their crowns before the throne. They are royal by association, choosing to submit to the King.[58] Above all, the throne room is a place of worship.

Read Revelation 5.

The Creator of the universe has finally set about to complete the restoration of his kingdom. And it all hinges on the reign of the promised King, who is the Seed and the Son (Rev. 5:13). There are two things I want you to look at in this passage of Scripture.

First, look at the description of the King. Rev. 5:5 describes the figure sitting on the throne as *"...the Lion of the tribe of Judah, the Root of David..."* All those titles should be ringing alarm bells in your head. They have served as flags, marking our path through the biblical story.

Here's a quick recap. In chapter 3, we learned that it would be through the tribe of Judah that the royal Seed would come (Gen. 49). In chapter 5, we learned that this promise of a coming, royal Seed would find fulfillment in the house of David. All these royal titles are combined with the image of a sacrificial lamb (Rev. 5:6) and link the King to the portrait of the Old Testament Messiah (Is. 53). In Revelation, the King is revealed to be the Passover Lamb, the Lion of Judah, and the Seed of David. There is no doubt that he is the Seed of salvation promised throughout the biblical story.

The book of Revelation reminds us that God is faithful to his promises. And because we serve a faithful God, we can trust him with our future. He has promised us the King will come once more to finish the work he has begun in our lives, and we have every proof he will keep his Word.

Second, look at the description of the King's kingdom. Among its inhabitants we see not just Israel, but people from all tongues, tribes, and nations. This is the masterpiece God intended when he created Adam and Eve for a restful life in his garden. This is the picture he painted for Abraham who would bear the promise of salvation to all people. This is the portrait God wanted his sons and daughters to become: priests to the nations. The King's kingdom is a place for all those who trust in him.

I don't know if you've ever had the chance to worship in another language. If you have, Rev. 5 springs to life. While my husband and I lived and worked in Southeast Asia, we attended a large non-denominational church. It included people from around the globe – Americans, Europeans, Singaporeans, Africans, Russians, and the list goes on. The church was a living embodiment of Rev. 5, people from all tongues and all tribes and all nations gathering to worship in many different languages.

In fact, my favorite services were the ones in which we sang familiar hymns like "Be Thou My Vision" and "Amazing Grace" in another language. Despite projecting the words onto a big screen for us, we still managed to butcher the words. But I cannot explain the depths of worship into which your heart is plunged when you hear those precious, familiar melodies cried out in a chorus of different tongues.

Talk about heightening your view of God! When you see the diversity of souls that God has created, redeemed, and is at work to restore back to his image, your view of his loveliness and grandeur takes a monumental leap skyward. If the final kingdom is a place where the King's servants perfectly reflect their King, then the throne room of the King will be unparalleled! It won't matter where you came from or what your past looked like, how well you can sing, what language you speak, what size dress you wear, or if you lived uptown or downtown or somewhere in the middle. The throne room will burst with Daughters of the King from different cultures and countries – all unified by the King.

The King Restores Rest through Judgment

We know from the biblical story God always intended his kingdom to be a place of rest. Revelation tells us that it is only through judgment that rest can be stored. Scripture is clear. Christ is coming again for his people to complete their restoration (1 John 3:2). But in order for the King's kingdom to be fully restored, all sin and evil must be removed first.

In chapter 2, we learned that the effects of sin touched all people and all of the earth. This is true still today. And so, the eradication of evil and sin must occur before God's creation – and we with it - can be completely and totally restored to him. We first started our tour of the biblical story in Genesis, discovering that God gave a significant promise to Adam and Eve regarding the coming Seed - a male figure who would crush the serpent and all evil (Gen. 3:15). This promise of restoration was paired with judgment.

Read Revelation 20.

Rev. 20 shows us what God's judgment will look like. All those who have rejected the gospel news of Christ - who are still dead in sin and found outside the kingdom – will reap the natural consequences of their choices. And while the King desires for all his daughters to come home, some will chose to follow their own path toward destruction.

The book of Revelation speaks of many different events occurring at the end of the age, but there are two actions God takes as part of his judgment.

The King defeats evil

First, all evil is defeated. Rev. 20:7-10 speaks of the beast, the false prophet, and Satan (the serpent of old) all coming under the judgment of our holy King. They find the same end as those who have placed themselves outside of the kingdom of God: They are thrown into the lake of fire. Because Christ is the eternal King, his defeat of Satan is eternal.

The King judges the nations

Next, Rev. 20:11-15 tells us that all those whose names are not written in the Book of Life will be thrown into the lake of fire as well.

God's judgment sounds appalling, doesn't it? We like to think of God as Love (and he is!), but God's holiness doesn't necessarily fit with the image we've constructed of God as an aging grandfather who spoils his loved ones and winks at bad behavior. When we cringe against the picture of God's wrath against sin painted by the apostle John, we are avoiding the confrontation that sin most assuredly brings. In order to be faithful to the full teaching of the Scriptures, we must be clear in even the most unpleasant of details. God clearly communicates to us what it means to be separated from him, and we see the horrific nature of that separation in this passage. It is against the horror of sin that God warned Adam and Eve in the garden, and it is for the horror of sin that Christ laid down his life on the cross.

For all those who choose to place themselves outside of God's reign, they will experience the curses of death. They will not and cannot be included in the kingdom of rest, a place where sin and evil are absent because it has been destroyed by the King.[59]

I share all of this with you not to intimidate you or scare you. Rather, the King's triumph over sin through judgment is good news for those who are found in him. At the time when we stand in the judgment, we will not be evaluated on our own works or our own devices; instead, we'll be judged by the work of Christ on our behalf (John 5:22; Acts 17:31; 1 Cor. 3:9-15). And while the Book of Life will most certainly contain a record of our activities on earth, our names are only entered into the book based on God's grace and by his very hand! (Ps. 87:6).

Only those of us who have entered into a covenant relationship with God and have chosen to live under his reign will be evaluated based on Christ's eternal righteousness. It is only by the name of Jesus Christ that our names, as his daughters, appear there.

THE KING COMPLETELY RESTORES ALL CREATION

So far, the message of Revelation has been difficult, even gory at times. It bothers our conscience that unbelievers will experience eternal separation from God, and it should.

Yet, we must understand, as Vaughan Roberts puts it that "judgment has a constructive purpose."[60] The destruction of evil is mandatory for the re-establishment of the restful rule of the kingdom. And the last two chapters of Revelation give us a glimpse at what this new, completed kingdom looks like.

Read Revelation 21:1-6.

Our journey through the biblical story ends here in these final chapters of the book of Revelation. I hope as we've taken this tour together, you've noticed a few things. Primarily, that the Bible is one, unified story all hinging on the person and work of the King and how the King goes about restoring us to his kingdom.

The passages I've selected have solidified that truth. Rev. 21:1-6 is no different. Did you notice that it employs similar language to another passage of Scripture we've studied? Isaiah 65:17 says, *"For behold, I create new heavens and a new earth; And the former shall not be remembered or come to mind."*

God promised to restore us. So, let's see how this final restoration stacks up to the promises given to the patriarchs.

God's People

All those whose names are written in the Book of Life (who have trusted in Christ and live under God's rule) will be called his people (Rev. 21:3). They will relate to God in unity once again – dwelling together in this new creation in rest, and there will be no pain or sorrow because evil has passed away (Rev. 21:4). God's people will inherit these blessings of life alongside Christ (Rev. 21:6).

But this restored kingdom is even better than life in the Garden of Eden. While Adam and Eve had fellowship with God, it was at a sub-regent level under God. It was restful and intimate. But those found in the body of Christ are now pictured as his bride! (Rev. 21:9; 22:17) You, as a Daughter of the King, are part of his chosen and cherished bride: the church.

I can't think of any relationship more intimate than the marriage relationship. You relate to your spouse with much greater intimacy than you relate to your parents, family, siblings, friends, and even your kids. This is one reason God gave us the marriage relationship and sanctified it as a holy picture of the unity between Christ and the church (Eph. 5). Our relationship in the kingdom will be even better than that which Adam and Eve experienced before sin. God's people in the restored kingdom will dwell in much more intimate way with God. Now we are more than just sub-regents, we are his beloved!

God's Place

Not only is our *relationship* with God in the restored kingdom going to be better, but our *location* will be better too! The Garden of Eden was beautiful indeed. But in Rev. 20 we see Jerusalem (remember it was called the City of God during David's reign) has also had a makeover. It is pictured in verses 9-21 as descending from heaven. John is clearly linking the final restoration of the earth to the idyllic state experienced by Adam and Eve before sin.

Did you notice the familiar language that is used to describe the Garden of Eden?

But key to the promise of land was the temple, a place where man might dwell (partially) in the presence of God in order to worship him and offer sacrifices of atonement. So, would you not expect to see a glorious temple shining in the center of the city? The prophets spoke of the glory of this new temple.

Read Revelation 21:3, 22-27.

No temple is needed. Just as the temple was no longer needed after Christ's death and resurrection, so no temple will be needed in the restored kingdom. The living tabernacle – Jesus Christ – permanently dwells with mankind in the New Jerusalem (John 1; Rev. 21:22).

As Daughters of the King we have unhindered access directly with our beloved King. Our worship and service to him will be face-to-face. There will be no more masks to disguise the contents of our hearts; our hearts will be completely transformed toward him. There will be no more hurried prayers, uttered as we enter into an unknown or painful situation; our life purpose will be to bring praises to he who found us and brought us home.

The temple, purposed to be a place for all nations to gather, is no longer needed because God's glory is the "light" for the people. Rev. 21:22-24 says, *"The city had no need of the sun or of the moon to shine in it, for the glory of God illuminated it. The Lamb is its light. And the nations of those who are saved shall walk in its light, and the kings of the earth bring their glory and honor into it."*

God's Rule and Blessing

From the very beginning, God's goal in creation was rest. His work culminated in rest, and his pattern for life in the kingdom involved mankind's restful service to God. And this pattern will not change with the new creation. In fact, restful, abundant life is the blessing that comes from living under God's rule. John paints a beautiful picture of this reality in Revelation 22.

Read Revelation 22:1-5.

I want to remind you how the author of Genesis described the first kingdom with such clarity, even speaking of life-giving rivers. Do you remember Ezekiel's prophecy of a river coming out of the new temple? (Ezek. 47:1-12) Since Christ is the temple, we should not be surprised to find a river of life proceeding from his throne. For all of us who have

114

trusted in Christ and follow his rule, we will receive the blessing of life from the King. Here's a glimpse of the abundant life that awaits us as Daughters of the King.

We finally will live restful lives (Rev. 22:1-2). We will have eternal life. Your life in the new creation will be different from what it is like today. Your life will not be characterized by worry, riddled with fear, or burdened by sickness. Your calendar will not be weighed down with never-ending bills, overwhelming responsibilities, or tedious busy work. Your days will not be filled with grumbling, slights, or injustices. Nor will your nights be filled with dread for the morning or remorse for the day's activities. Instead, your life will be a life of restful worship and service to the King.

We finally will be freed from sin (Rev. 22:3-5). We will be freed from the sins plaguing our lives. You will no longer make the wrong choices. You will no longer snap when your kids ask you a question or respond angrily to your husband. You will no longer be debilitated with guilt over past mistakes or trapped in negative internal dialogues. Instead, you will be set free from sin's disastrous consequences, and you will be free from sins committed against you. You will no longer have to deal with pain, worry, poverty, injustice, brutality, war, or hunger. You will no longer ask yourself: *"What did I do wrong?"* Or the more insidious question: *"What could I have done better?"* Whatever it is you are dealing with today, that is threatening to drown your heart in fear and anxiety - divorce, broken friendships, relationship failures, addictions, pride – they will all be totally wiped away in the new creation. They will no longer exist, and you won't remember them anymore.

CONCLUSION

Despite this glorious vision, John ends the book of Revelation, and so God's story for the earth, with a warning. Rev. 22:12-17 warns us that Christ is coming again and sooner than we might expect. His judgment on sin will complete the restoration process.

Rev. 22:12-17 says, *"And behold, I am coming quickly, and My reward is with Me, to give to every one according to his work. I am the Alpha and the Omega, the Beginning and the End, the First and the Last. Blessed are those who do His commandments, that they may have the right to the tree of life, and may enter through the gates into the city. But outside are dogs and sorcerers and sexually immoral and murderers and idolaters, and whoever loves and practices a lie. I, Jesus, have sent My angel to testify to you these things in the churches. I am the Root and the Offspring of David, the Bright and*

Morning Star. And the Spirit and the bride say, 'Come!' And let him who hears say, 'Come!' And let him who thirsts come. Whoever desires, let him take the water of life freely."

Do you notice how all our themes of the kingdom in the biblical story find their end in this passage?

God's People: *God's covenant with man is made possible through his eternal Son* (Rev. 22:12), who is the son of David as fulfilled by prophecy (Rev. 22:16).

God's Place: *God's covenant with man finds it location in his eternal Son* (Rev. 22:13). And until Christ comes again, we live with a foretaste of our eternal home with the indwelling of the Spirit (Rev. 22:17a).

God's Rule and Blessing: *God's covenant with man reaps blessings of eternal life if we submit ourselves to the Son's rule* (Rev. 22:14, 17b). And those who choose to remain outside of the kingdom will reap the natural consequences of sin (Rev. 22:15).

I hope this study of what it means to be a Daughter of the King has helped you discover where you are located on the biblical timeline and your place in God's story for the world. God has a mighty plan for you. You are his chosen and cherished bride, whom he has tasked with the great responsibility to be a light to the nation. The biblical story identifies you, as the King's daughter, as a priest, co-heir, and co-ruler of the King's kingdom, titles which are eternally based on the faithfulness of our forever king who sits on his forever throne.

My Story:

Above all things, dear Daughter of the King, I hope you take the following truths to heart.

As a Daughter of the King, I am an essential member of the King's kingdom – as God's People, in God's Place, living under God's Rule.

Each of us who have trusted in Christ and follow his rule will receive the blessing of life with the King. As Rev. 22:12-17 tells us, we should be watchful for Christ's return and expectant for our ultimate restoration from sin. We should live our lives with forward-looking eyes – hopeful and expectant for the time when all our present circumstances and sufferings are erased, when we will finally be at rest.

As a Daughter of the King, I have a special role to play in the King's plan for restoring the world – a role as both priest and worshipper.

In looking to the future, the biblical story makes it clear that the way we live now matters. The "here and now" is incredibly important to the kingdom. As a Daughter of the King, the way you live and the degree to which you are faithful to your King either helps draw others into the kingdom or encourages them to remain in darkness. Ultimately, the decision to enter into the kingdom of Christ lies with the individual presented with the invitation and not us. We can trust the Spirit of the King to guide those souls who have been invited to approach the throne safely home. Yet, out of the King's grace, he gives you and me a special role to play in that process.

As Daughters of the King, we are given a precious task: to serve the King by being a light to the nations. We are to imitate Christ in our daily lives so that others might be drawn to the King and into his kingdom.

The Bible is the most important story we will ever hear. It is also the most lovely and life-changing story ever written. Without, it, we would never understand our distinctive purpose or exceptional worth as the King's daughters. Without it, we would never see the precious meaning behind the circumstances in which we now walk. Without it, we would never know that a good King created a good world, and although it was corrupted by sin, he is at work to completely restore it through His Son, Jesus Christ.

One day, the King will return for his daughters. Come, Lord Jesus. Until then, let our kingdom story shine.

"He who testifies to these things says, 'Surely I am coming quickly.' Amen. Even so, come, Lord Jesus! The grace of our Lord Jesus Christ be with you all. Amen." (Rev. 22:20-21)

Chapter 10: The Kingdom at Rest

1. How many of the promises made to Abraham does Christ fulfill?

2. The book of Revelation paints a vivid picture of the King when he returns at the end of the biblical story to restore his kingdom. Describe the King in Revelation 5:5-12. (Consider who he is, where he is sitting, what his subjects are doing and saying about him).

3. The book of Revelation also describes the King's kingdom as it will be when it is finally restored. According to Rev. 5:13, what does this final kingdom look like? Consider who inhabits it and what they are doing.

4. How does the King restore rest to all creation and us - as his daughters? (Review Rev. 20 if needed).

5. In this study, we've discovered that the Bible is one, unified story all hinging on the person and work of the King and how the King goes about restoring us to his kingdom.

If someone were to ask you to summarize the story of the Bible – and your role in it - in 30 seconds, what would you say?

ABOUT THE AUTHOR

Melissa's motto as a Christian journalist and creative writer is to "tell of God's marvelous works" (Ps. 9:1). And with almost 15 years of experience in print and editorial services, God has embedded Melissa with passions gleaned from stories and experiences from the field.

But helping women fall in love with the sweetness of God's Word truly makes her heart sing. Two years ago, she launched HiveResources.com to help women sweeten their walk with Christ through Bible study, ministry and missions resources, and more.

Melissa has a M.Div. in Women's Studies from Southeastern Baptist Theological Seminary, Wake Forest, N.C., and a B.A. in Journalism from Texas A&M University.

She and her husband, Jonathan, are part of a church plant in Pittsburgh, Pennsylvania. They have five-year-old twin boys, Zacharias King and Jonah Joseph, who are unwittingly and joyfully shaping them into the image of Christ.

NOTES

1 Unless otherwise indicated, all Scripture cited from the NKJV. All emphasis is mine.

2 Vaughan Roberts, *God's Big Picture: Tracing the Storyline of the Bible* (Downers Grove: Intervarsity Press, 2002), 21.

3 As stated in the introduction to this study, the definition for the kingdom of God is taken directly from Vaughan Roberts's book (see above citation). For more books that delve into the larger story of Scripture, check out the following titles by Graeme Goldsworthy: *According to Plan: The Unfolding Revelation of God in the Bible, Preaching the Whole Bible as Christian Scripture,* and *The Gospel and Kingdom.* Also consider the following titles by Craig G. Bartholomew and Michael W. Goheen, *The True Story of the Whole World: Finding Your Place in the Biblical Drama* and *The Drama of Scripture: Finding Our Place in the Biblical Story.*

4 Vaughan Roberts.

5 John Sailhamer, "Man's place in the garden (2:15-24)" in *The Expositor's Bible Commentary*: Vol. 2 (Grand Rapids: Zondervan Publishing House, 1990), 45.

6 John Sailhamer "The temptation (3:2-7)" in *The Expositor's Bible Commentary*: Vol.2 (Grand Rapids: Zondervan Publishing House, 1990), 51.

7 Wendy Alsup, *The Gospel-Centered Woman* (CreateSpace Independent Publishing Platform, 2013), 23.

8 John Sailhamer, "Exile (3:22-24)" in *The Expositor's Bible Commentary*: Vol 2 (Grand Rapids: Zondervan Publishing House, © 1990), 59.

9 Vaughan Roberts, 51.

10 David Jones, "Lecture 5b." Lecture, Marriage and Family from Southeastern Baptist Theological Seminary, Wake Forest, NC, Fall 2006.

11 John Sailhamer, *NIV Compact Bible Commentary*, (Grand Rapids: Zondervan, 1994), 76.

12 Charles Brand, Charles Draper, & Archie England, *Holman Illustrated Bible Dictionary* (Nashville: Holman Reference, 2003), 1428.

13 Vaughan Roberts, 72.

14 R. Laird Harris, "The Annual Sin Offering of the Day of Atonement (16:1-34)" in *The Expositor's Bible Commentary*: Vol. 2 (Grand Rapids: Zondervan Publishing House, 1990), 587. Harris writes, "Clearly the Day of Atonement was to symbolize for Israel every year the substitutionary atonement God provided for their sins and the total removal of their guilt."

15 Vaughan Roberts, 68.

16 Walter C. Kaiser, Jr., "Collection of materials (25:1-9)" in *The Expositor's Bible Commentary*: Vol. 2. (Grand Rapids: Zondervan Publishing House, 1990), 453. According to Kaiser, sanctuary means "holy" place or "the place set apart." The word "tabernacle" (Heb. *mishkan*) is derived from the word "to dwell" (Heb. *shakan*), the place where God dwells among his people (cf. 29:42-46; Lev 26:9-12; Ezek 37:26-28; Rev 21:2-3). Kaiser writes: "The most important word about the sanctuary was that it was to be built according to the "pattern" God would show Moses. The word "pattern" (Heb. *tabnith*) comes from the verb "to build" (Heb. *banah*). This word signals the fact that typology is present, for this is only a "model" or "pattern" of the real thing (see v.40)."

17 For further proof that loyalty to God was a heart issue, see Josh. 23:11.

18 Charles Brand, Charles Draper, & Archie England, *Holman Illustrated Bible Dictionary* (Nashville: Holman Reference, 2003), 985-986.

19 Charles Brand, 985-986.

20 Frank E. Gaebelein, *The Expositor's Bible Commentary*: Vol. 3 (Grand Rapids: Zondervan Publishing House, 1992), 888-890.

21 Frank E. Gaebelein, 892.

221 Paul Tripp, "David's Dying Words," http://paultripp.com/wednesdays-word/posts/davids-dying-words-3.

23 Daniel L. Akin, *Theology for the Church*, (Nashville: B&H Academic, 2007), 199.

24 Chart adapted from Vaughan Roberts, *God's Big Picture: Tracing the Storyline of the Bible* (Downers Grove: Intervarsity Press, 2002), 91. Not included in this chart is the prophet Jonah, who prophesied directly to the Assyrians living in Nineveh during the 8th BC, and Habakkuk, a book recording a dialogue between the prophet and God around 586 BC. For dating according to Assyrian, Babylonian, and Persian dominance see J. Daniel Hays, *The Message of the Prophets: A Survey of the Prophetic and Apocalyptic*

Books of the Old Testament (Grand Rapids: Zondervan Publishing House, 2010), 35.

25 Geoffrey W. Grogan, "The Deliverance of the Lord's Remnant (10:20-34)" in *The Expositor's Bible Commentary*: Vol. 6 (Grand Rapids: Zondervan Publishing House, 1986), 84.

26 Geoffrey W. Grogan, "The Man of Sorrows and His Vindication (52:13-53:12)" in *The Expositor's Bible Commentary*: Vol. 6 (Grand Rapids: Zondervan Publishing House, 1986), 303. Grogan believes the language of Is. 53:6 could possibly derive from the Day of Atonement ritual in which the high priest symbolically transferred the sins of the people to the scapegoat (Lev 16:21-22; Lev. 17:11).

27 Geoffrey W. Grogan, "The thematic approach to Isaiah" in *The Expositor's Bible Commentary*: Vol. 6. (Grand Rapids: Zondervan Publishing House, 1986), 18. Grogan points out that the dominant use of the first person singular in the later two suffering servant songs. Grogan writes: "He is taught, he suffers, he is vindicated, and he imparts God's truth to others, who are judged by their attitude to him. There is not, in fact, in the third and fourth songs a single expression necessitating or even suggesting that the servant is a group rather than an individual."

28 Vaughan Roberts, 100.

29 Cf. Daniel 7.

30 Cinderella Illustration adapted from a sermon by Michael L. McCoy, "The Garments of Salvation: Isaiah 61:10 - 62:37," found at www.scholia.net.

31 See D.A. Carson, "The Genealogy of Jesus (1:1-17)" in *The Expositor's Bible Commentary*: Vol. 8. (Grand Rapids: Zondervan Publishing House, 1984), 61-66.

32 John Sailhamer, *NIV Compact Bible Commentary*, 437.

33 D.A. Carson, "The temptation of Jesus (4:1-11)" in *The Expositor's Bible Commentary*: Vol. 8. (Grand Rapids: Zondervan Publishing House, 1984), 112-114. In his commentary, Carson offers a wonderful explanation of how Jesus's victory over Satan's attempts at temptation act as a test just as Israel was tested. Carson also demonstrates various parallels with historic Israel 40 year-stay in the wilderness and Jesus' fast of forty days and nights reflected Israel's forty-year wandering (compare with Deut 8:2-3). Carson makes a link that the purpose of the parallel is to prove and appoint a

worthy son of God and underscores the theme of royal kingship.

34 Merrill C. Tenney "The Incarnation of the Word (1:14, 16-18)" in *The Expositor's Bible Commentary*: Vol. 9. (Grand Rapids: Zondervan Publishing House, 1981), 33.

35 Merrill C. Tenney, 33.

36 Be sure to check out Merrill C. Tenney's historical look at the importance of Christ acting as a life-giving temple. In his commentary (see earlier citations), he offers an insightful look at the context in which Jesus made this claim, namely the Feast of Tabernacles, established to memorialize the wilderness wandering when the people had little food and water. Tenney writes that "the celebration of the Feast of Tabernacles included a daily procession of priests from the temple to the Pool of Siloam, from which they drew water that was poured out as a libation at the altar. This was accompanied by the recital of Isaiah 12:3: 'With joy you will draw water from the wells of salvation'." According to Tenney, Jesus's words here act a reminder of God's promises all along the biblical story and a call to faith.

37 Leon Morris, "The Blood of Christ (9:11-14)" in *The Expositor's Bible Commentary*: Vol. 12. (Grand Rapids: Zondervan Publishing House, 1981), 85.

38 John N. Oswalt, *The Book of Isaiah: Chapters: 40-66* (William B. Eerdmans Publishing Company: Grand Rapids, 1988), 626. Oswalt says, "They are not the sign of new life coming, but of the lack of conception, because all they do is self-serving and self-enhancing (cf. Is. 57:12; 58:2)."

39 Vaughan Roberts, 124.

40 Walter Liefeld, "The appearance to the disciples (24:36-49)" in *The Expositor's Bible Commentary*: Vol. 8 (Grand Rapids: Zondervan Publishing House, 1984), 1057-58. Liefeld points out that the power of the Spirit - the "power from on high" (*ex hypsous dynamin*) – is revealed from the very beginning of Luke's Gospel narrative (i.e.: Luke refers to the Spirit's role in the virgin birth in Luke 1:35).

41 For a more exhaustive treatment of the various roles and activities of the Spirit, see Michael Reeve's *Delighting in the Trinity: An Introduction to the Christian Faith* (IVP Academic, 2012).

42 Considering that the only Scriptures available to the early church at the time were the Hebrew Scriptures, Peter demonstrates what apostolic

teaching would have looked like – interpreting the Law and Writings through the lens of Christ's death and resurrection.

43 Is. 49, *"It is too small a thing that You should be My Servant To raise up the tribes of Jacob, And to restore the preserved ones of Israel; I will also give You as a light to the Gentiles, That You should be My salvation to the ends of the earth."* See also the book of Ruth and Jonah for God's love for all nations and Israel's role to reach them.

44 Vaughn Roberts, 132.

45 Vaughn Roberts, 132. (cf. 2 Pet. 1:1-3)

46 Edwin A Blum, "Christ the Rock and the Christian living stones (2:4-8)" in *The Expositor's Bible Commentary*: Vol. 12. (Grand Rapids: Zondervan Publishing House, 1981), 229-231. In his commentary, Blum points out that Peter applies to the church the title of priest originally spoken to Israel (Ex. 19:5-6; Deut. 4:20; 7:6; Is. 43:20-1). See Romans 11 for help in understanding the differences that remain between Israel and the church, because as Blum explains, the church in no way replaces Israel or becomes Israel, as God still has glorious plans in place for his chosen people. Blum writes: "In the future, according to Paul, God will once again use Israel to bless the world (cf. Rom 11:1-16, 23-24)...The title "chosen people" stresses God's loving initiative in bringing the church to himself."

47 Charles Brand, Charles Draper, & Archie England, *Holman Illustrated Bible Dictionary*, 1328

48 Charles Brand, 1328.

49 Charles Brand, 1328.

50 Edwin A Blum, 229-231.

51 Another Pauline Epistle written to Titus (a Gentile to whom Paul left to lead the church in Crete) on how he should instruct the church concerning salvation (by grace alone) and godly living. I appreciated Hiebert's insight into the phrasing of the original language "might become heirs," which he notes is not just a future prospect but a present reality. See D. Edmond. Hiebert, "Its basis (3:5a)" in *The Expositor's Bible Commentary*: Vol. 11 (Grand Rapids: Zondervan Publishing House, 1978), 445-446.

52 John H. Sailhamer, *NIV Compact Bible Commentary*, 527. "Abba" is Aramaic word.

53 Peter O'Brien, *The Letter to the Ephesians: The Pillar New Testament Commentary* (Leicester: Apollos, 1999), 135.

54 Peter O'Brien, 136.

55 Find out more about the Vinton's ministry at http://www.villageschools.org/.

56 Alan F. Johnson, "General Nature and Historical Background of Revelation" in *The Expositor's Bible Commentary*: Vol. 12 (Grand Rapids: Zondervan Publishing House, 1981), 400-401. The word "revelation" is literally *apocalypsis* in the original Greek.

57 Alan F. Johnson, 400-401. In his commentary, Johnson underscores the purpose of suffering in the life of the believer. He writes, "In Revelation the climactic event has already occurred in the victory of the slain Lamb (Rev. 5). Now, however, the Lamb's victory is being worked out in history in the obedient suffering of his followers (Rev. 12:11; 15:2). Their deaths are seen in Revelation as a part of the victory over evil that God is already affecting in the world. This partial victory through the suffering of the saints is combined with the hope of the final unambiguous victory of God at the end of history."

58 Alan F. Johnson, 4614. Johnson states, "While the 'crowns of gold' are likewise usually related to the redeemed, here they refer to the royal dignity of those so closely associated with the throne of God (cf. 1 Kings 22:19; Ps 89:7). Golden crowns are referred to in 4:4, 10; 9:7; 14:14."

59 Vaughan Roberts, 144.

60 Vaughan Roberts, 146.

Made in the USA
Columbia, SC
15 November 2019